MILLENNIALS
and MISSION

D0843622

I first met Jim in the early 70's while he was working with a "Jesus movement" church on the University of Minnesota campus. He was warm, passionate, and totally dedicated to making Jesus known. We lost track of each other for years, but in the meantime he went on to serve in missions, led WEC-US and then began teaching intercultural studies to new generations of young college students who had interest in missions. Jim teaches at Bethany College of Mission and has helped our faculty and mission team better understand this Millennial generation—and how to better engage with them to reach all people everywhere with the gospel of Jesus Christ.

What has impacted me about Jim is that forty years later from when we met, he is still Jim. He is "warm, passionate, and totally dedicated to making Jesus known." And, he loves this Millennial generation that God has placed before us. Will we step forward to disciple, love, invest, and launch them? Will we not just tell them what they need to know, or will we say "come with us" and walk with them as we "do the kingdom, not just talk about it?" Jim is a doer of the kingdom—in his family, in the classroom, and in taking the Great Commission literally. *Millennials and Missions* is a wonderful and vibrant appeal and road map to serving this next generation—they will lead in the future. (We actually don't have any choice about that.) So let's invest all that we have into them—let's love them—let's serve them—let's launch them.

Daniel H. Brokke
president/CEO, Bethany International
Bethany College of Missions

Missionaries know all about the importance of contextualization when it comes to the gospel—that is communicating the unchanging truths of God's call of salvation in culturally relevant forms so that it is not only heard, but understood. In this important work, Jim and Judy Raymo provide all of us who care about the Great Commission with a necessary reminder that we must also contextualize the call to missionary involvement. This book will help you understand and reach the hearts of the next generation of would-be cross-cultural workers—the Millennials.

Stan Guthrie
author, *Missions in the Third Millennium*

Jim and Judy Raymo have lived out the Great Commission in their lives. They have incarnated their love for Christ and the world through their efforts locally, globally, and with their family. Read this book and hear of their heart for Millenials, missions, and ministry in our world. You will not be disappointed by what you learn and how you are impacted.

John Jackson, PhD
president of William Jessup University

This book should be read by the entire missional community. My prayer is that every person in the silent generation/builders and boomers will read this book and learn what it takes to encourage this exciting generation to reach the world with the Good News.

Tom Telford
church mobilizers serving with United World Mission

Every generation confounds and mystifies its predecessors. Thus, "paradoxical," the key word Jim and Judy Raymo have chosen to describe Millennials, is both an insightful and a hopeful summary. Their analysis is incisive while avoiding pigeon-holing and caricatures. At its core, this book tells a hopeful story, propelled by the Great Commission, that this generation brings many correctives, a host of connective skills and tools, and a creativity to tackle formidable obstacles to the gospel. You will be encouraged as you read of the energy, the iconoclasm, and the passion of this generation of Christ-followers. Prepare to have your stereotypes shattered. God is still in the business of deploying his disciples!

Roger Thompson
senior pastor, Berean Baptist Church

MILLENNIALS and MISSION

A GENERATION FACES A GLOBAL CHALLENGE

JIM and JUDY RAYMO

WILLIAM CAREY
LIBRARY

All scripture quotations, unless otherwise indicated, are taken from the Holy Bible, New International Version®, NIV® copyright ©2011 by Biblica, Inc.™ Used by permission of Zondervan. All rights reserved worldwide. www.zondervan.com. The "NIV" and "New International Version" are trademarks registered in the United States Patent and Trademark Office by Biblica, Inc.™

Scriptures quotations marked "ESV" are taken from The English Standard Version® (ESV®) copyright © 2001 by Crossway, a publishing ministry of Good News Publishers. All rights reserved. ESV Text Edition: 2011.

Scripture quotations marked "NASB" are taken from the Amplified® Bible, copyright © 1954, 1958, 1962, 1964, 1965, 1987 by The Lockman Foundation. Used by permission. (www.Lockman.org)

Scripture quotations marked "NLT" are taken from the Holy Bible, New Living Translation, copyright © 1996, 2004, 2007 by Tyndale House Foundation. Used by permission of Tyndale House Publishers, Inc., Carol Stream, IL 60188. All rights reserved.

Scripture quotations marked "NKJV" are from the New King James Version®. Copyright © 1982 by Thomas Nelson, Inc. Used by permission. All rights reserved."

Published by William Carey Library
1605 E. Elizabeth Street
Pasadena, CA 91104 | www.missionbooks.org

Melissa Hicks, editor
Brad Koenig, copyeditor
Josie Leung, graphic designer
Rose Lee-Norman, indexer

William Carey Library is a ministry of the
U.S. Center for World Mission
Pasadena, CA | www.uscwm.org

Printed in the United States of America
18 17 16 15 14   6 5 4 3 2 SFP

Library of Congress Cataloging-in-Publication Data

Raymo, Jim.
    Millennials and ministry : a generation faces a global challenge / By Jim and Judy Raymo.
        pages cm.
    ISBN 978-0-87808-536-1
    1. Church work with youth. 2. Church work with young adults. 3. Generation Y--Religious life. I. Raymo, Judy. II. Title.
    BV4447.R37 2013
    259'.23--dc23
                            2013038481

CONTENTS

FOREWORD

From Genesis to Revelation the Bible is one book with one theme. What God began with scattering the nations in Genesis 11 he completes in Revelation 7. There *will be* a representative from every tribe, tongue, people and nation worshiping him. Expanding God's Kingdom is the responsibility for every generation of believers and every generation brings new opportunity and new obstacles. It is no different with today's Millennial generation. As we pass the baton to the members of this unique generation, it is critical that we understand the opportunities and obstacles they face.

Literally, no generation before has had the world at its fingertips quite like this one has. Technological advances are mind-blowing. Global access is instantaneous. Information abounds to an almost paralyzing degree. How will Millennials respond? Will they get off the couch and engage or hibernate into their smartphones? One thing is sure - those of us who mentor them can help light the way to involved engagement. To do this we must gain all the insight and understanding we can. Only then can we move strategically forward. This is exactly what Jim and Judy Raymo provide.

I met the Raymos before they met me. In 2001 I read their first book, *Marching to a Different Drummer*. I was new to the mission world and was captivated by their ability to distill difficult topics into simple, transferable and applicable steps. It quickly became my favorite missions book. When I had the pleasure of meeting them in person I realized they were more than just great authors. Their hands-on ministry of raising up laborers to the unreached was equally impressive.

In *Millennials and Missions* they have done it again. Ever since the term "Millennials" has been coined, the Raymos have been involved in not only researching them but reaching them. They have a passion to figure out how to mobilize Millennials and activate them to the mission of God. You hold in your hand their expertise. Mobilizing a generation is a daunting task. The Raymos give us a roadmap to do just that.

Todd Ahrend, PhD
international director, The Traveling Team
author of *The Abrahamic Revolution* and *In This Generation*

ACKNOWLEDGMENTS

We want to express our appreciation to those who assisted and encouraged us in the process of putting this book together. The editing and graphing help and recommendations of Kathy Hoffmann, Leif Masrud, and Todd Ahrend were critical. The Millennial blog responses and conclusions by Shasta Feltman were a vital contribution. The wisdom of Dr. Tom Correll, Dr. Garry Morgan, and Dr. Nils Friberg provided especially helpful assistance and insight. Above all, we thank the Lord for His strength and perseverance to complete both the doctoral dissertation and its conversion into this book.

INTRODUCTION I

For more than forty years, I have enjoyed the privilege of getting to know and serving with missionaries—or should I say, cross-cultural workers? The mere choice of a term can denote generational difference.

My initial exposure to missions came about in an unusual fashion. I grew up in a non-Christian home and was drawn to faith in Jesus while in the US Army. As a combat engineer platoon leader in Vietnam, I first encountered missionaries with the Christian and Missionary Alliance. I was struck by the bravery of these workers, seeing them as perfect, selfless people. Although they would flinch at being called perfect, they seemed to have a high purpose and an inner drive to bless and care for the Vietnamese in Jesus' name. God planted missions in my heart at that early stage of my Christian life. I knew nothing of the concept of a calling, but I am certain the commitment those missionaries exhibited was the result of God's leading/calling in their lives. I was inspired to pursue God's purpose for me.

Over the years my wife and I have worked in local churches and global missions in a variety of roles. Presently I teach worldview and cross-cultural ministry courses at a Christian college. In the past we lived and worked for seven years in London, Frankfurt, and Amsterdam, witnessing to and discipling young Europeans. This was followed by six years of team pastoral and teaching ministry with a church on the University of Minnesota campus.

After we joined WEC International in 1987, we both taught at the mission's training college and led orientation courses in the USA, Australia, and Canada, preparing aspiring missionaries for cross-cultural work. Then we served as the USA Directors for WEC for six years. That responsibility gave me opportunity to visit many countries. Seeing churches pioneered by missionaries, engaging in prayer and dialogue with national leaders, and worshiping in a variety of contextual forms fascinated and inspired me. Of course, as anyone who has served in ministry in this country or overseas is aware, problems and disappointments occur. People do not always come into line or respond as we think they should. But it is very evident that God continues to build His church around the world.

Working with the Millennial generation in recent years, I have been intrigued by its mix of strengths and weaknesses. These young people are the future of ministry. I have looked for opportunities to study and understand them further. I found such an opportunity when I was considering a topic for my doctoral dissertation. The conclusions which form the foundation of this book are drawn from generational sociologists, surveys, interviews, research, and personal experience. My wife has attempted to weed out the "academese" of my dissertation and added more narrative elements. Additionally we included blog comments from a representative of the younger generation. I trust the result will be interesting and informative for those considering a ministry career as well as for those attempting to motivate others to join the adventure.

A significant portion of my focus has been on suitability for and attitudes toward cross-cultural work based on my years working in mission contexts. Increasingly as the book has developed, and I have thought through my time in pastoral ministry and college teaching as well, I have found the conclusions applicable to ministry in general, at home or abroad.

Ministry opportunities and challenges are becoming increasingly multicultural, as well as multigenerational, requiring a blend of aptitudes and attitudes for successful work. Global influence and interaction are on the rise. North American communities are receiving growing numbers of immigrants from many ethnic backgrounds. Here in Minnesota, our children's school rosters are filled with names like Nour, Carlos, Adonte, Khalid, Edriss, Dayana, Aziz, Esmail,

Ovidio . . . any shopping trip or workout at our local "Y" includes the sound of several languages besides English and the sight of neighbors wearing distinctly different cultural dress. The skills, attitudes, and characteristics mission agencies consider as they seek to mobilize and train new workers for cross-cultural ministry overseas are increasingly the same qualities needed for work in our churches, schools, and other ministries here in North America.

Jim Raymo

The authors can be contacted at jjraymo@msn.com with any questions or comments concerning this book.

INTRODUCTION II

I grew up in the Lutheran church in Southern California. There I came to faith in the Lord Jesus and dedicated my life to His service before I was in my teens. Over the intervening fifty years, I've actively participated in a "Jesus Movement" university church, an interdenominational mission, and several "nondenominational" and Baptist churches here and overseas, but I confess that I remain a Lutheran at heart. Martin Luther is one of my heroes. Luther was a flawed human being, with views and outlook influenced by the worldview of his culture and times, six hundred years ago. The Lord did not strike him with a lightning bolt (well, almost—but that's another story) and instantly change each and every less-than-holy way Luther thought or saw the world. He remained an imperfect person, yet God was able to use him to change the course of the church, make His Word available to ordinary people, and initiate the wave of Protestant missions.

What God accomplished through Luther should encourage us all. Whatever generation we come from, whatever our culture—Boomer, Xer, Millennial—none of us is infallible. We have much to learn, but God can use us if we step out in obedience and faith.

Jim wanted me to issue an apologetic for why my stories and illustrations often mention WEC. So please note clearly that I am not saying WEC is the best mission, and I am not saying other missions aren't the best! I simply know WEC the best. I will say—heads up, Millennials! For a century-old, originally British mission, WEC is a surprisingly good fit for you.

Judy Raymo

MILLENNIALS: A GENERATION UNLEASHED?

Over the years as I have worked alongside, trained, led, and learned from younger people in Europe, Australia, Canada, and the USA, I have been inspired, bewildered, amused, and frustrated (as I am certain they have been with me!) by their challenging contributions. Throughout this journey I have sought to understand and respond intelligently to generational differences. My aim in this book is to explain what I have learned in the process, particularly in the context of cross-cultural ministry.

The Millennial generation (born 1982 to 2002) in North America is being introduced daily to a growing and tumultuous level of pressures and threats. Every generation faces challenges, struggles, and danger. What perhaps makes this generation's situation unique from those of the past is its overly optimistic expectations and immediate exposure to global events.

How will this generation of Christians respond to both dangers that seem pervasive and the global biblical mandate to go to all nations with the teachings and life of Jesus? Will fear and overwhelming desire for safety rule its choices? Will protecting family, job security, advanced health care, and retirement funds be seen as necessary insurance for a future without pain? Will disturbing challenges be seen as opportunities for the church to demonstrate its core ethos and sacrificial roots, or as difficulties to be avoided?

> I'm a bit of a nutter, so bear with me, but after every question I want to give a passionate, emphatic, "No! No! We will prevail! We will go! We will serve, we will sacrifice, we will LOVE." This is our battle cry! Yes, I'm ready God!

Let's go. I'm ready to serve the poor and feed the hungry, comfort the outcast, go to the hard places." (all said in my head, of course, I'm comfortable, sitting in an American coffee shop) *Shasta Feltman, Millennial Blog*

Historically the church has stepped up and demonstrated what it proclaimed, that Christ lived out a sacrificial life and death and calls His people to do the same. Comments by Kristin Kobes Du Mez illustrate this:

A series of devastating plagues played an instrumental role in the seemingly miraculous growth of the early church . . . Contemporary accounts describe widespread panic as family members abandoned their loved ones at the first sign of disease, sometimes tossing them into the roads even before they had died . . .

Christians, however, soon gained a reputation for their boldness in the face of death . . . the bishop Dionysius, for example described how Christians showed unbounded love and loyalty, never sparing themselves and thinking only of one another. Heedless of danger, they took charge of the sick, attending to their every need and ministering to them in Christ and with them departed this life serenely happy: for they were infected by others with the disease, drawing on themselves the sickness of their neighbors and cheerfully accepting their pains.

I was struck by the contrast between the sacrificial behavior evidenced by early Christians and the reputation of many American Christians today. Looking back over recent American history, it is discouraging to note how fear, rather than selfless sacrifice, often seems to have motivated Christians to act.[1]

The response of the early church to the plagues differs sharply from the church's initial reaction to the contemporary crisis presented by the HIV pandemic. Rather than offering compassion and selfless

---

[1] Kristin Kobes Du Mez, "Plagues, Terrorism, Recessions and Christian Witness," http://www.gospelandculture.org (accessed November 23, 2010; site discontinued).

help, the evangelical church tended to condemn the victims and treat them as outcasts. Panic and shunning of those within the church who suffered from HIV reflected the general public's confusion and fear.

One of the saddest commentaries on the church and this crisis is found in the book *Burden of a Secret* by Jimmy Allen, former president of the Southern Baptist denomination. His daughter-in-law contracted AIDS through a blood transfusion and passed the disease on to her two infant sons before the family realized she was ill. Allen's son was on the staff of a church in Colorado. Seeking counsel and consolation, he met with the senior pastor to inform him of the family's illness. He was asked to resign immediately. Additionally,

> We suspected that someone who attended the church and also worked in the hospital had spied the family's health records and had spread the word that the Allens had AIDS. In a matter of days, both Scot and Lydia were unemployed . . . Lydia was asked to remove Matt from the church daycare center. The family was asked not to return to the church.[2]

After their baby son died of AIDS, no Christian school would accept their kindergartener. Only a public school finally agreed to educate their older son, Matt.

> Lakewood Elementary School, a public school, exemplified far more of the Spirit of Christ than did many of the institutions that bear his name. It wasn't that the people of Lakewood did not have their fears and reservations about a child with AIDS. But where there was fear, they overcame it. Where there was ignorance or confusion, they sought to provide the truth. For instance, when Mrs. Marian Hammert, Matt's kindergarten teacher at Lakewood Elementary School, was told an AIDS child would be in her classroom, she knew so little about the subject that she had to have a special briefing . . . At the end of Matt's first year of school, however, Mrs. Hammert came to our

---

[2] Jimmy Allen, *Burden of a Secret: A Story of Truth and Mercy in the Face of AIDS* (Nashville: Moorings, 1995), 66.

family members and said, "I love Matt so much. If there is any problem next year, I am also qualified to teach first grade. I would be glad to shift grades to be his teacher."[3]

What a tragic role reversal from the church's earlier heroic sacrificial responses to crisis! We all feel fear when threatened. I found myself facing fear of AIDS when in the process of adopting one of our sons, we were told his birth mother was HIV-positive at the time of his birth. My first response was that we should withdraw. I told my wife, "I would never want to have an AIDS child in our family who might infect the rest of us. We would probably be simply housing him to usher him to his death." As I thought about this before the Lord, I recognized my fear was really more about what others would think of us and how they would treat us.

My wife's logical and compassionate response was twofold: the little boy had been tested throughout his first year and had not shown any evidence of the disease, but even if he should have the virus, whose responsibility is the care of these children if not Christians'? We ended up going ahead to adopt Daniel, who at the time of this writing is ten years old, healthy, and a lively addition to our family.

In the face of numerous global crises including the HIV pandemic and international terrorism, will the younger generation step up to care for its neighbors and to share the gospel in life and words? Will self-protection be their legacy, or will the Christians of this generation set self-interest aside and offer themselves to extend the kingdom of God?

After my first book[4] was summarized in an *EMQ* article,[5] I was engaged in a radio interview addressing call-in questions from listeners. A parent posed this question: "Are you really seriously suggesting that

---

[3] Ibid., 115.

[4] Jim Raymo, *Marching to a Different Drummer: Rediscovering Missions in an Age of Affluence and Self-interest* (Fort Washington, PA: Christian Literature Crusade, 1996).

[5] Jim Raymo, "Reflections on Missionary Malaise," *Evangelical Missions Quarterly* (October 1997): 442–46.

we release our children to places around the world that are dangerous and without all the benefits we've built in America?" Yes, I am serious. Is this question the normal response of the Christian population? With millions of people, here and abroad, still untouched by the gospel, and in the face of many "dangers, toils, and snares," will this generation hesitate because of fear and worry or obey the Great Commission and move forward confidently because Jesus said, "Go"?

WHO ARE THE MILLENNIALS?

We are both Baby Boomers and currently have three Millennials living in our home. (We defer to them on all matters involving technology!) Our youngest son didn't make the Millennial cutoff, while our older children belong to Generation X. Our experience confirms what sociologists report: generational differences are real and may be observed in a variety of social encounters.

For example, we Boomers grew up with "hit the bat" or "three flies up" in the street as our main athletic experience. When our first three children were young and began participating in team sports, trophies were handed out at the end of the season. Some were labeled "Most Improved," others "Hardest Worker" or "Best Sport," etc. Finally the coveted "Most Valuable Player" trophy would be presented. To their disappointment and mine, none of my kids ever received that award, but they always cheered for the teammate who did.

Years later when one of our younger boys played his first sport and received his award on the last day, I looked down and swelled with pride: he held the "Most Valuable Player" trophy! I began to congratulate him, but then I heard another dad nearby congratulating *his* son on earning the "Most Valuable Player" trophy! As I glanced around, I saw that every child was holding an MVP trophy. Unthinkable that any little Millennial's self-esteem might be damaged by a hint that he or she wasn't the best!

A November 2007 segment on *60 Minutes* titled "The 'Millennials' Are Coming" presented an insightful, but not always flattering, picture of this generation's work habits and lifestyle. The program asserted that although they know how to surf the Net and engage with people around the world through the Web, many young career seekers have never punched a time clock or been required to fulfill work goals in a timely manner. They are poorly equipped to handle disappointment. A commentator concluded, "They were raised by doting parents who told them they are special, played in little leagues with no winners or losers, or all winners. They are laden with trophies just for participating, and they think your business-as-usual ethic is for the birds. And if you persist in the belief, you can take your job and shove it."[6] I've shown this video to over four hundred college students, who frequently comment, "That's us!"

How can we understand a generation that has grown up indulged and protected from life's disappointments and failures? How will the Christians of this generation face adult life, responsibility, an entitlement culture, and the challenge of ministry in an uncertain world?

Attempting to understand Millennials might be compared to looking at a tapestry: the various influences and factors are best viewed as a whole, from a distance. When one part of the tapestry is examined up close and in isolation, confusion and wrong conclusions may result. Viewing "snapshots" of this generation's characteristics is necessary for understanding, but the "big picture" should be kept in mind when studying each detail. Research to date has been concentrated on Millennials from North America. Although cogenerationists from other parts of the world may share some of the same influences and characteristics, there are also many factors that differ according to culture, socioeconomic situation, available education, etc.

Generalizations about Millennials suffer from the same fate as any generalizations: as soon as one is made, an exception pops up. So of course, conclusions about the group won't necessarily apply to any individual within the group.

Millennials, born between 1982 and 2000, show a mixed bag of strengths, weaknesses, and idiosyncrasies. They've shared significant

---

[6] CBS News, "The 'Millennials' Are Coming," *60 Minutes*, February 11, 2009 (originally broadcast on November 11, 2007), http://www.cbsnews.com/stories/2007/11/08/60minutes/main3475200.shtml (accessed May 2, 2009).

life events at critical developmental stages, with the events of September 11, 2001, deeply influencing their worldview. The sheer size of this generation makes it important sociologically and culturally. In the USA, "Population statistics indicate that, as of 2006, Millennials between the ages of 18 and 24 reached 28.2 million, and they are projected to reach 30 million by 2010."[7] This immense group is entering its peak years for employment and careers, making them a serious generational force to reckon with. They represent the most diverse North American generation to date, with 38 percent of eighteen- to twenty-four-year-olds coming from minority ethnic backgrounds.

Perhaps unwittingly, the parents of these young people have contributed to the making of a group that has been called "Generation Me." "Baby on Board" signs accompanied the arrival of these cherished children. Smaller nuclear families and the threats (real and perceived) of contemporary life meant many of them grew up with "helicopter parents," who hovered about with zealous care and the anxious desire to make their children's lives perfect. Mom and Dad did all they could to guard and protect young self-images from failure or embarrassment and intervened to smooth out any problems. The result, according to researcher Raina Kelley, is the creation of "a generation of hothouse flowers puffed with a disproportionate sense of self-worth and without the skills they need when Mommy and Daddy can't fix something."[8]

Childish self-absorption and a sense of entitlement have been strengthened by parents' impulse to give their kids whatever it takes to make them happy. One conversation among moms I (Judy) volunteer with at our local elementary school concerned a four-year-old who had been so upset that her nine-year-old sister got a new iPod Touch (worth about $350) that the parents decided to hurry out to get one for the preschooler, too. The other parents seemed to think this was perfectly normal and unremarkable and discussed the special features

---

[7] Darlene E. Stafford and Henry S. Griffis, "A Review of Millennial Characteristics and Military Workforce Implications," CNA, http://www.cna.org/sites/default/files/research/d0018211.a1.pdf (accessed May 22, 2013).

[8] Raina Kelley, "Generation Me," *Newsweek*, April 4, 2009.

of their kids' iPods and iPhones. (I kept quiet—and was glad our iPod Touch-less thirteen-year-old wasn't around.)

One aspect of this younger generation to keep in mind throughout is their relative immaturity. Their nickname "The Boomerang Generation" reflects the fact that many choose to return to live with their parents after college, seeing this as a wise economic decision. As a result they tend to achieve independence and move into marriage and parenthood later than other generations. Supervisors and job coaches see late-adolescent young people today as four to six years behind the previous generation in sociological and psychological development. The reasons for this delay may include media saturation that allows them to live in a fantasy world, being raised in an environment of prosperity, parental concerns for safety, and numerous choices in an information-rich environment.

Millennials seem to recognize their own inclinations: "A Harris Interactive poll found that twenty-one to thirty-one-year-olds were voted the most greedy and self-indulgent even by the twenty-somethings themselves, who were actually more likely than the older generations to agree that the young generation had these narcissistic tendencies."[9] The CNA study cited previously reported: "Millennials are generally very self-critical, rating their generation as 'most greedy' and 'most self-indulgent.' They most admire the Baby Boomer generation and call Gen X 'most productive.'"[10]

> Ouch . . . and probably a bit true. I don't even know what to say. Um, I think we're a pretty resourceful bunch— maybe emotionally immature, but maybe we're just more open about airing our problems instead of stuffing them: hiding them. There is a lot of pressure to perform, create successful lives and live up to the expectations of our parents—they pour money, time and love into our early lives to give us the best chance of success. So we enter life with paradoxical expectations: It's all about us and we

---

[9] Jean M. Twenge and W. Keith Campbell, *The Narcissism Epidemic: Living in the Age of Entitlement* (New York: Free Press, 2009), 34.

[10] Stafford and Griffis, "Review of Millennial Characteristics."

must succeed; make our mark, but we haven't had failures to temper our idealism with wisdom. *SF, Millennial Blog*

Surveys completed by these recent college students suggest that this generation is more selfish, less interested in the well-being of others, and less concerned about the environment than was expected.

The entitled me-first attitude is not the only characteristic noted by generational researchers. Hope, resiliency, and tenaciousness also describe this group:

> Millennials are reversing the long-term direction of change—the delta of history. Today's kids are doing this so dramatically that, as a group, they are behaving better than their parents did as kids—and better than many of the parents (or leaders) behave even now, as adults. And they are doing it against a demoralizing riptide of negative examples from many of the same adults who lecture them so fiercely.[11]

In both of the Christian colleges I have been associated with, I have found this generation to be basically friendly, usually rule following, and serious about achievement. My students are a thoughtful, somewhat impulsive group, enamored with technology and staying in touch with friends through texting and Facebook. They encounter the same types of temptations and challenges as previous generations, but also have an ever-available wealth of information no other generation could instantly access.

Socially they tend to be a self-correcting force. In one class I (Jim) had a student who repeatedly entered the room late, just as I was beginning to teach. He would walk to an empty seat, making comments to those around him, possibly to be noticed or produce a laugh. Finally one day, another student looked up as he was doing this and said loudly enough for everyone to hear, "Shut up! He is trying to start." That was the end of the problem. Occasionally I need to speak to an unruly student, but often others in a class provide a corrective restraint.

---

[11] Neil Howe and William Strauss, *Millennials Rising: The Next Great Generation* (New York: Vintage Books, 2000), 17–18.

Researchers have found that the group values "Timeliness, Making a Difference, Tolerance, Environmental Stewardship, Authenticity, Family, Global Perspective, Personal Freedom, and Technology."[12] These translate into three major areas of aspiration.

First, Millennials share a desire to transcend the natural, material world. For some, this takes the form of appreciation for the undefined mystery of the cosmos. For others, this means searching for a spiritual element in life, exemplified in the "Personals" section of the University of Minnesota daily paper where students place adds looking for someone who is SBNR: Spiritual but not Religious.

Second, they want significance and feel that a person's life should be meaningful and purposeful in the eyes of others.

Third, they look for community and a sense of family in the midst of a fracturing world and society. The type of loyalty and enduring friendship (often including readiness to "bed-hop") demonstrated by the television series *Friends* represents the quintessential expression of community to them.

> Critical thinking was hammered into us by the educational system—at least those of us who were paying attention— and now the word on all of our lips is "why"? Why do we have to do it that way? Why can't life be fun, why can't work be enjoyable? Why can't we sit on couches and love our co-workers, why can't we work hard and build community? We question, we evaluate, we try new things, we're flexible and have an aspiration to pair community with efficiency and effectiveness. *SF, Millennial Blog*

Every generation is deeply affected by those that have gone before. For instance, my generation, the Boomers, frequently reacted to the Builder generation's characteristics and goals such as loyalty, conservatism, patriotism, and an affluent lifestyle. Researchers list readily-accessible birth control, legalization of abortion on demand,

---

[12] Carol Philips, "The Millennial Handbook: A Snapshot Guide to Everything Gen Y," Brand Amplitude, http://www.brandamplitude.com/Millennial_marketing/Millennial_marketing.html (accessed September 12, 2009; page discontinued).

the zero-population-growth movement, increase in divorce rates, more mothers in the workplace, and movies as the most significant influences passed on to the Millennials from Generation X.[13] Comparing descriptions of the major characteristics of each recent generation can help in understanding the current group of young adults.

Chuck Underwood summarizes them this way:

The Silents, born between 1927 and 1945, came of age deferring to the more assertive preceding G. I. Generation. They were North America's "last innocent" group. Their formative years were an era of extreme conformity, as well as the post–World War II happy days: Peace! Jobs! Suburbs! Television! Cars! Rock 'n Roll! The first hopeful drumbeats of civil rights! This generation provided the iconic leaders of the 1960s' social revolution. Many Silents are working past normal retirement age and have excelled in the helping professions. They are a RIGHTS generation.

The Boomers, born between 1946 and 1964, are an amalgam of two distinct subsets: the save-the-world revolutionaries of the 1960s, followed by the self-improvement partyers of the late '70s and '80s. They are career driven and known as the "Golden Generation" in the American workplace. They are assertive, ethical, and demanding, but have struggled with marriage and parenting. America will be a Boomer-led nation into the 2020s. This generation is all about VALUES.

GenX, born between 1965 and 1981, are latchkey kids who grew up street-smart but isolated, often with divorced or time-starved, dual-career parents. They are entrepreneurial, independent, and creative. Government and big business mean little to them. They often feel disempowered and disengaged. They are eager to make marriage work and to "be there" for their children. This generation is all about SURVIVAL.

Millennials, born between 1982 and 2000, are a sharp departure from Generation X. They are optimistic, idealistic, patriotic, and carefully supervised. They revere the wisdom of elders. They are

---

[13] William Strauss and Neil Howe, *Generations: The History of America's Future, 1584 to 2069* (New York: Morrow, 1991), 12.

team players and tend to still be redefining life in their twenties—an extended adolescence. They are not yet loyal to employers and are delaying marriage and parenting. They want to be about ACTION.[14]

> Reading Underwood's generational description is like reading a personal bio . . . yikes Batman! Spot on. "Optimistic, idealistic, they revere the wisdom of elders . . . redefining life in one's 20's . . . delaying marriage and parenting" (mostly). I suppose this may be true of any generation passing through this stage of life, but I wouldn't know. I'm twenty. *SF, Millennial Blog*

MILLENNIAL FACTS

❑ 2010 Pew Research describes Millennials as "confident, self-expressive, liberal, upbeat, and open to change."

❑ 75 percent have profiles on a social network, while 20 percent have uploaded a video of themselves to the Internet.

❑ Almost 40 percent have at least one tattoo, and 25 percent have a body area other than their ears pierced.

❑ 37 percent of eighteen- to twenty-nine-year-olds are unemployed or out of the workforce (this includes those going to school who are not employed; without school, the unemployment rate was 14.4 percent, compared to the national rate of 8.5 percent).

❑ 66 percent claim "you can't be too careful" when dealing with people, but they are less skeptical of government than previous generations.

---

[14] Chuck Underwood, *The Generational Imperative: Understanding Generational Differences in the Workplace, Marketplace and Living Room* (North Charleston, SC: BookSurge, 2007).

- ❏ 60 percent were raised by both parents, the lowest rate of any generation so far.
- ❏ 20 percent are married (Boomer marriage rates at this age were double this).
- ❏ 33 percent are parents.
- ❏ 40 percent age eighteen to twenty-four are enrolled in college.
- ❏ 39 percent over twenty-two are living with their parents again (the "boomerang" generation).
- ❏ 2 percent are military veterans.
- ❏ More identify themselves as liberal, not supportive of a strong national security policy, and backing more progressive social policies than other generations.
- ❏ 83 percent sleep with their cell phones.[15]

In general, this generation is more racially and ethnically diverse and more "tech savvy" than older generations. In regard to faith, Millennials in significant numbers have moved away from the religious affiliation of their childhood. They are more likely than the general population to identify themselves as being unaffiliated or holding nontraditional beliefs. Less than 25 percent believe the Bible is the word of God and should be taken literally, with nearly 40 percent stating the Bible is only a book written by men. Although the majority says Christianity has "good values and principles" and "consistently shows love for other people," almost two-thirds believe that Christianity can be described as "anti-gay" and "judgmental."[16]

---

[15] Kat Southard, "The Millennials," MAVANetwork, January 10, 2012, http://mavanetwork.wordpress.com/2012/01/10/the-millennials/ (accessed January 15, 2012).

[16] Robert P. Jones, Daniel Cox, and Thomas Banchoff, *A Generation in Transition: Religion, Values, and Politics among College-age Millennials; Findings from the 2012 Millennial Values Survey* (Washington, DC: Public Religion Research Institute and Georgetown University's Berkley Center for Religion, Peace, and World Affairs, 2012), http://publicreligion.org/site/wp-content/uploads/2012/04/Millennials-Survey-Report.pdf (accessed July 7, 2012).

If we were to choose one word to describe Millennials, that word would be "paradoxical." This is a generation comfortable with paradox, two or more realities that seem contradictory. They agree with Ralph Waldo Emerson that "a foolish consistency is the hobgoblin of little minds." The following list provides insight into the members of this group and how teachers, leaders, pastors, and employers can help:

They are sheltered, but pressured. Millions of these students have been sheltered from harsh realities by their parents, yet they live with more pressure on their lives than the previous two generations. Our response? Help them to simplify their lives as much as possible and set clear, understandable goals.

They are self-absorbed, but generous. They spend more time in the morning getting ready for the day than Generation X and the Baby Boomers, and they spend more money on themselves as well, even when you factor in inflation. However, these students give their time and money away at a much faster pace. In fact, you might say they see money as "easy come, easy go." They love giving and helping others, once their own needs are met. Our response? Expose them to needs in their community or around the world in developing nations and challenge them to expand their horizons.

They are social, but isolated by technology. They are in constant contact with peers and family through text messaging, cell phone calls, IM, Facebook, MySpace, and all sorts of Internet networks. The irony is, they are also the most isolated bunch of students, because so much of their relational contact is via technology. Their people skills are poor, and most struggle with handling difficult people. Our response? Create face-to-face relationships with them, as well as peer communities where they meet in person.

They are adventuresome, but protected. Parents have monitored almost everything. Often, each level of school has only prepared them for more school. Our response? Enable them to take control of their lives. Allow them to set their priorities and warn them that they'll live with the consequences of their decisions.

They are team-oriented, but diverse. These kids have grown up playing soccer on teams and performing school projects in groups. Yet they are the most racially diverse generation in modern American history. Our response? Work with them to appreciate strengths in others.

They are visionary, but vacillating. We see this all the time. These young people will capture a passion for something—and get caught up in a vision for becoming involved in an organization to make the world a better place. Yet the vision is fleeting. It loses its novelty quickly. As one dean said to me, "These students want to change the world, but before the week is over, they've changed their minds." Our response? We must help them remain focused on one major priority at a time, and keep commitments for a set length of time.

Their orientation is high achievement, but high maintenance. This is a confident, optimistic generation of kids. They require lots of attention, feedback, and rewards from authorities. Our response? As much as possible, we must provide consistent feedback, at least in the beginning.[17]

Young people seem to be aware of some of the paradoxes they display, and apparently they can live with them. They are critical and demanding regarding the behavior of leaders, while at the same time admitting they cheat on their schoolwork and paint a picture of themselves via social media that often stretches the truth. They are caught between their own me-first attitude and expectations, their idealism and sense of themselves as people who can make meaningful achievements, and their parents' desire that their children gain in tangible ways from their expensive investment in a college education.

> I can't speak for all of us, but I think it's safe to say that we're disillusioned with three-story houses and parents with expensive cars but crumbling marriages. But we're also the product of prosperity so we're wrestling with that, too. We're polite and considerate but wild at heart,

---

[17] Tim Elmore, "A Generation of Paradox: The Strange Contradictory Characteristics of Generation Y." Growing Leaders. http://www.growingleaders.com/index.php?home (accessed May 23, 2008; page discontinued).

incredibly educated but rejecting the careers that let our parents pay our tuition. We carry iPads and wear designer shoes, but we bike to work and donate our extra cash to famine victims in East Africa. What a strange bunch we are. *SF, Millennial Blog*

When considering who Millennials are, the effect of technology on their lives and character cannot be overemphasized. Seeing one of them without iPod or iPhone in hand is rare indeed. It's difficult to count the number of times a student focused on texting while walking through a college building has nearly run me down. Texting is this group's means of constant communication, with its own dialect and rules. They take for granted the instantaneous nature and feedback of the latest electronic devices. They confidently use every type of new technology.

As the CNA study concluded,

> The most popular new technologies are those that allow Millennials to always be connected, without anchoring them down, which explains why text (and Facebook) messages have replaced email as the preferred methods of personal communication for this generation. Millennials tend to be as demanding of their technology as they are of themselves, and for this reason, are more likely to wonder why they haven't always had new technologies than to marvel at the way things "used to be." Even "luxury" electronic items like iPhones are seen as "necessities" for many Millennials, who can't imagine life before computers.[18]

Warnings concerning technology are increasingly being sounded by those who study the cognitive and decision-making processes of young people. Growing up in a world of video games, websites, and iPods is creating a generation that goes through its days isolated from others, earbuds plugged in, barely registering what is happening outside its electronic gadgets. Despite continual texting and Facebooking, Millennials struggle with interpersonal relationships and exhibit

---

[18] Stafford and Griffis, "Review of Millennial Characteristics."

weakness in face-to-face communication skills. Facebook, blogs, and YouTube have in fact opened a Pandora's box of communication without accountability. This generation, as Feuerback wrote, "prefers the image to the thing, the copy to the original, the representation to the reality, appearance to being."[19] Although he was writing in 1843, this is a fundamental Millennial characteristic.

The global, digital world has a growing impact on cross-cultural mission strategy. Ministry organizations lean increasingly upon the latest electronic equipment to fulfill their goals. Promisingly, these young people are "first adapters"—not afraid to try newly developed technologies—and they quickly learn to operate each new innovation.

Attitudes regarding the use and appreciation of all things technical have evolved. Traditional cell phone usage is now similar across generations, but Millennials lead in the use of newer phone/Web instruments. They understand the technology intuitively and are pleased to train older generations in its use. Can we dinosaurs humble ourselves to learn from younger techies? Our four sons, ages ten to twenty-one, seem to know instinctively how to comfortably navigate computers and the Internet in ways we still have to take painstaking step by painstaking step.

These young people are filled with hope, ideas, and zeal, but planning ahead to fulfill their dreams and passions is frequently missing. In college classes, students often speak of hopes for the future, including involvement in missions and humanitarian efforts, but they have failed to make any provision for taking the steps necessary to achieve their aims. Leaving essential steps to chance or a naïve grasp on "God's will" frequently results in frustration and disillusionment. Many Millennials seem to lack the real-world knowledge and acumen to move their plans from step A to step D, or from aspiration to completion.

Contrary to some opinion, Millennials are not purposely disrespectful towards older generations. Their tendency to ask why things

---

[19] Christine Rosen, "The Image Culture," *The New Atlantis* 10 (Fall 2005): 45.

are done a certain way seems to be translated as disrespect and disregard for tradition. In my experience these young people demonstrate respect in different ways and for reasons other than simply acknowledging a title or position. For example, when meeting new applicants as USA director of WEC International, I found their tone of voice and body language, though not particularly disrespectful, to be laid back and informal. My title obviously did not impress them. They did not know me. If over time I was able to connect with them and their hearts for Jesus, I would notice their demeanor towards me changing. Relevance to their lives caused them to see me as an authentic leader deserving of respect from within rather than a token nod because of my position in an organization.

In contrast, when I would meet Korean applicants for the mission, the respect and honor for leaders built into their culture was evident from the first introduction, typically demonstrated by respectful body language, including bows on occasion, and willingness to remain listening attentively until dismissed.

This young North American generation has been raised with a strong sense of entitlement, believing they are special and exceptionally good problem solvers. They depend on positive feedback for their efforts. Parents and society have protected them to a greater extent than any other generation. From car seats to lockdown drills, safety has been paramount, and they expect the same protection from organizations they might join. They are confident that following college, an employer (or mission agency) will help unleash their potential for greatness. Their lives have been heavily scheduled since childhood, with technological devices to keep track of athletic events and dance lessons and with pressure to succeed academically in anticipation of a rewarding career. These young people want to work on teams and expect a leadership structure more egalitarian than in previous generations. They expect a clearly defined job description. They appreciate constant affirmation and compliments on their performance.

> This is a big deal—if we don't feel attached or valued by an organization, why should we care about them? We want continuity between work and family—not a separate "everybody does what's best for them" attitude. If you're going to give your life to a company/agency, then it must mean something to you—you must care about your co-workers and peers and they must care for you outside how much you produce or contribute. *SF, Millennial Blog*

As the Millennials look toward the future some feel anxiety about changing work and ministry environments. They are influenced by the implications of globalization including personal and family safety in a world threatened by increased terrorism. Some express concern about negative perceptions of missionary paternalism and cultural insensitivity shown by Americans in the past. They have a reluctance to impose their own beliefs on others but are adamant about working in a ministry context that is holistic. They have inherited unparalleled worldwide opportunities due to today's ease and speed of travel, instant communication, and many open borders. How do their expectations, character traits, and habits suit them (or not) to take advantage of these resources to carry out the Great Commission?

INSPIRING A GENERATION

Several years ago Patrick Johnstone, author of *Operation World* and research director for our mission, and I were traveling to a mission mobilization meeting. Because his book is widely used, Patrick has numerous opportunities to speak with Christian organizations about God's global activity. He mentioned that he was finding the younger generation requires not simply information on statistics and needs to motivate them, but also inspiring personal stories and an understanding of the biblical basis for missions expressed in narrative form.

I agreed that awakening an awareness of God's work through missions and motivating Millennials to join that work must include sharing real life stories as well as presentation of a solid biblical foundation. For instance, young people anxious about the possible dangers and limits of serving in "closed" countries are intrigued by stories like the one we heard from two men who were transporting Bibles and study materials in the local language to a small city in a restricted-access nation, where workers' names are not publicized for security reasons. Apparently during their bus trip, a plainclothes policeman observed them talking about their destination and phoned ahead to have the local police detain the young men and examine their bags.

As the two stepped down from the bus, they were taken into custody and led to the police station, where their bags were emptied and the contents scrutinized. The Christian literature was confiscated and placed in stacks on a table nearby. The men were ordered to sit down and wait until the judge arrived. They were certain this would result in jail time and loss of all their ministry materials. As they sat praying and hoping for deliverance, the guys noticed that local people coming into the station would quietly approach the table and examine the Bibles and other items. One after another would pick up a Bible or book, glance around to be sure no police were observing them, slip the literature into a pocket or inside a coat, and quickly leave.

When the judge finally arrived, he was told the men were being held for "proselytization." He asked to see the contraband literature. A policeman went to the table, but found that every piece had disappeared. Nothing was left. The police frisked the two men, but found nothing on them and were left empty-handed before the judge, who angrily told them to release the prisoners since, "You and I have more important work to do."

The workers left, free and rejoicing that God's Word had penetrated areas of the city they would never be able to reach on their own. God's promise that He will build His church and the gates of hell will not prevail against it was fulfilled in the presence of two young missionaries. Millennials respond eagerly to authentic stories like this that illustrate God's grace, protection, and power.

I believe a strong biblical case for missions can be presented to the younger generation based on five foundational points.

First, evangelism, discipleship, and church planting remain necessary goals for fulfilling the Great Commission from Matthew 28:20.

Second, large numbers of people around the world still have no immediate access to Christians or a church.

Third, although non-Western believers are becoming increasingly involved and are leading many areas of the mission enterprise, the church in the West continues to be needed as a partner in reaching the world. There is plenty of work for all.

Fourth, the authority for missions comes from its initiator, God Himself.

Fifth, the holistic expression of the gospel favored by Millennials is exactly the direction in which mission organizations are moving, joining practical expressions of the love of God with proclamation of His truth.

Sometimes I wrestle with this: what makes me so special, what gives me the right as a person from the West to go and be the "savior" to a lost people? Gosh, that's so cliché d. Yuck. But first, I'm not the Savior. OK, so you probably already caught that one. But still, what gives me the right? Why me? Because I'm an American, because I have an education? Because I know better? Because I've had training? Because I'm part of the majority? Because I'm saved? Someone call the police, it's all so cliché d— and quite frankly, wrong. Are we just doing this because it's noble? Or do we really care? Can we ever have pure motives, is that even the point? Sheesh, I ask a lot of questions. Welcome to my head, yes it's exhausting. There's a lot of pain and suspicion out there. A lot of opinions. A lot of ideas about ministry—I think the term "missions" has really lost its meaning. Do we even know why we do it? Just sounds like a good idea, doesn't it? Seriously dude, it's a problem. *SF, Millennial Blog*

Apparently we have some way to go to help Millennials recognize and accept the real reasons for missions and their own responsibility to reach out to the world! Initially we need to help them understand that the *missio Dei* (mission of God) begins with God the Father Who sent the Son, not with us. Jesus told His followers that as the Father had sent Him, He would send them. After His resurrection, the Holy Spirit was sent to indwell believers so they could be sent into the world to make disciples of all nations. The *missio Dei*, the going and sending in order to bring people into relationship with Him, is what God does. We are given the privilege of participating in what He is doing.

Though many people assume missionary activity began with the Great Commission, the Bible demonstrates repeatedly, beginning with Genesis, that mission was in God's heart from the beginning. Even as He first began to form a set-apart people through Abraham, His intent was to reach out to every nation. As David Bosch explains, "God is a missionary God . . . To participate in mission is to participate in the movement of God's love toward people, since God is a fountain of sending love."[20]

From the beginning God's intention has been to touch all the nations with His goodness and power. He indicated this to Abraham (Gen 12:1–3) and promised that "Abraham shall surely become a great and mighty nation, and all the nations of the earth shall be blessed in him" (Gen 18:18 ESV). The New Testament explains that this promise of God has been actualized through faith (Rom 4). God has provided for the redemption of the entire creation including complete authority over the enemy (Luke 11:15–23). Jesus instructed His followers to look beyond their own home and people. His purpose was to change their parochial mindset to a "go into all the world" perspective that would result in "a great multitude that no one could count, from every nation, tribe, people and language, standing before the throne and before the Lamb" (Rev 7:9).

Historically the church has vacillated between activism and passivism in regard to reaching the world with God's redemptive message. At times the church has become preoccupied with its position and development and missed the imperative to go to the ends of the earth. Once when Israel became too concentrated on itself, God intervened through a prophet to reiterate one of His main purposes for the nation's creation: "It is too small a thing for you to be my servant to restore the tribes of Jacob and bring back those of Israel I have kept. I will also make you a light for the Gentiles, that my salvation may reach to the ends of the earth" (Isa 49:6). Jesus reinforced this purpose when He explained that "this gospel of the kingdom will be preached in the whole world as a testimony to all nations" (Matt 24:14).

The church, Jesus' body on earth, has inherited this commission to fulfill God's plan. However, before Jesus gave His "go" command, He instructed His followers to wait before the Lord to learn to move in His strategies. Faced with barriers created by visa restrictions and

---

[20] David Jacobus Bosch, *Transforming Mission: Paradigm Shifts in Theology of Mission*, American Society of Missiology Series, no. 16 (Maryknoll, NY: Orbis Books, 1991), 1–11.

political and military upheaval in the twenty-first century, the church needs a new vision and willingness to seek specific direction from the Lord. As Carl F. H. Henry explains,

> What modern Christians often forget is that fulfilling the mission to the nations is a Spirit-directed effort in which the risen Lord remains sovereign over evangelical witness and momentum. The evangel it proclaims requires all generations' engagement.[21]

"Open" and "closed" doors did not stop the growth of the early church. Fear of persecution, lack of amenities, concern for personal safety, and historic resistance to the gospel have contributed to slowness in reaching some areas and people groups. Missionaries have tended to go where people are responding to the Christian message, rather than digging in for the long haul among difficult populations. But the commission to go into all the world includes attempting to bring His truth to the least evangelized wherever they may be. As Jesus said, "I have other sheep that are not of this sheep pen. I must bring them also. They too will listen to my voice, and there shall be one flock and one shepherd" (John 10:16).

In the early 1970s a few WEC missionaries headed off to Spain to begin ministering. They faced strong resistance against "evangelicals" in this staunchly (and medieval-y) Roman Catholic country. None of the strategies used successfully on other fields seemed to work. Years went by with no visible results, and there seemed to be an impenetrable wall that couldn't be broken through. Eventually the team began to notice that the extremely few Spaniards who responded to their message were drug addicts. They started to wonder if the Lord might be showing them *His* strategy for Spain and started to concentrate their efforts among the population of addicts. These people, many suffering

---

[21] Carl F. H. Henry, "Theology of Mission and Changing Political Situations," in *Theology and Mission: Papers and Responses Prepared for the Consultation on Theology and Mission, Trinity Evangelical Divinity School, School of World Mission and Evangelism, March 22–25, 1976*, ed. David J. Hesselgrave (Grand Rapids: Baker Book House, 1978), 279.

from AIDS, poverty, homelessness, and despair, began eagerly responding to the care and hope offered to them in the name of Jesus. Today the Betel Church in Madrid, led by former addicts, is the largest evangelical church in Spain, and the drug treatment and vocational training programs begun there are now operating in many other countries as well. Allowing the Holy Spirit to show *His strategy* for ministry opened doors nothing could close.

Those who study the history of Christian missions often reflect on scriptures—such as "The plans of the LORD stand firm forever, the purposes of his heart through all generations" (Ps 33:11)—that focus on God's sovereignty. The church has an inconsistent record in applying this concept to the missionary commission. At times there has been an inappropriate application of the doctrine of God's sovereignty that has resulted in passivity towards reaching the world. A classic example of this followed William Carey's writing and presentation of "An Enquiry into the Obligation of Christians to Use Means for the Conversion of the Heathen" to a board of English Baptist leaders in 1787. Carey hoped to promote enthusiasm for ministry to the unreached, but to his consternation was harshly refuted. When he gave his address, John Ryland Sr. instructed him, "Sit down, young man. You are an enthusiast! When God pleases to convert the heathen, He will do it without consulting you or me."[22]

This reprimand served only to spur William Carey on in his zeal for missions. Since his day, the church worldwide has come to understand the call of the Great Commission and the need to use "means" to accomplish it. Two centuries of Protestant missionary activity, based upon verses like "We are therefore Christ's ambassadors, as though God were making his appeal through us" (2 Cor 5:20), have seen the gospel transported to every continent.

In our day, the perceived failures and paternalism of historic missions and the social and cultural changes commencing with

---

[22] William David Taylor, "Portraits: William Carey," The Baptist Page, http://www.siteone.com/religion/baptist/baptistpage/Portraits/carey.htm (accessed January 16, 2010; site discontinued).

postmodernism have prompted Christian young people to take a fresh look at negotiating life in relation to their role and responsibility regarding the Great Commission. They struggle to integrate the fact that in God's kingdom evil has been defeated even while the present state of the world is chaotic. They wonder how to reconcile the gospel's promised peace and victory with questions of evil and suffering. This juncture should be precisely where God's sovereignty spurs the church to action, not passivity. For Christians the sovereignty of God does not encourage fatalism, which believes things are as they are and cannot be changed, but rather the confidence that having discovered God's instructions and guidance, we can step forward in obedience knowing that He is ultimately in control.

One of the most daunting challenges facing the mission enterprise today is, of course, the growth of Islam. In contrast to the Christian concept of God's sovereignty, "Islam generally teaches that 'all good and evil comes from Allah,' so the sovereignty of Allah becomes a kind of fatalism for most Muslims. Undeniably there are Muslims who are active in the promotion of their faith by any means, including violence."[23]

In contrast, Christians see God's sovereignty in His prevenient grace to the human heart: His work in us before we sought or were interested in Him. Evangelism, discipleship, and church-planting efforts involve workers cooperating with God to bring His truth to those who are open and seeking. Acting as His ambassadors, we are privileged to communicate and demonstrate the gospel with love and graciousness, never with force or violence, knowing that we plant and water but God gives the growth.

Another area of challenge is the importance of holistic ministry. Mission events like Urbana have begun to emphasize the role of caring for the sick and dying, comforting the widow and orphan, and

---

[23] At a State Department briefing for mission directors, I learned that violent jihadists make up only about 1.3 percent of Muslims, although 10–15 percent are quietly supportive of their methods. Assuming one accepts the State Department figures, nearly 85 percent of Muslims disdain terrorism in the name of Islam. But 1.3 percent of 1.3–1.5 billion Muslims represent well over a million people who see violence as a legitimate means to their ends. A daunting thought.

working for justice along with sharing the message of redemption and discipling believers. The world needs to see the life of Jesus permeating every aspect of human existence. Millennials are particularly drawn to ministry that meets not only spiritual needs, but practical ones.

In 1992 people we knew generally reacted as if it was quite odd that we were adopting a child of another race who had serious medical issues. Now in 2013, international, interracial, and special-needs adoptions have become a rallying cry of the church. Many Christian leaders and celebrities speak and blog about the need for orphan care, while many churches have formed adoption and foster-care ministries and support groups. The human need of children around the world has been brought into the spotlight, and the church has taken up this cause with a new urgency. Ministries to street children and children traumatized by war, as well as campaigns against human trafficking, are other examples of holistic gospel ministry.

Contextualization is yet another vital aspect of the Great Commission. A proper approach to contextualization, with a balance of biblical faithfulness and cultural understanding, provides an environment in which God's mission can flourish. WEC's international leaders, concerned about the balance between biblical integrity and cultural sensitivity, formulated the following:

> Contextualization seeks to present the Gospel in word and deed to the end that a church is established in ways that people understand within their own local cultural context. The Gospel should be presented in such a way that it meets people's deepest needs and penetrates their worldview, allowing them to follow Christ and remain within their own culture, transforming it by the Gospel truth.
>
> The mission of God is always embodied in a specific culture, demonstrated in the Word having "become flesh." This does not mean that God has been absent from the culture before the arrival of those human agents bearing the good news. What it does mean is that the approach of the church must always be one of seeking to discover how God is already at work in the culture and then engaging in

serious reflection about how best to participate in this divine activity in ways that are culturally sensitive, relevant, life-giving and transforming. Cultural insiders are the best equipped to make choices about cultural forms.[24]

This approach to contextualization is biblically sound as well as pragmatically applicable in cross-cultural settings. Being learners in a new culture often comes more easily to Millennials than to those of previous generations, whose emphasis was often on delivering a message rather than on understanding appropriate contextualized communication.

> We don't want to be arrogant; we don't want to make the same mistakes of ethnocentrism and colonial-style missions. Valid concerns—those people tend to wreck havoc in the name of Jesus. But, I mean we REALLY don't want to be those people—we're really critical (going off of the sorts of conversations I had in ministry classes at college or out and about with my buds) and we go out of our way to be accommodating—overanalyzing our methods of ministry. I love this quote my friend Joe posted on his wall the other day:

> "Our most effective missionaries go to another country, learn their culture, and use that culture to bring people to God. When it's missionaries we call that effective. When we do it at home, we call it compromise."—Perry Noble. Then another person commented: "I remember Michael (missionary kid friend of ours) saying something like this to me—really made me think . . . because if I'd be all for dressing like the native people in China, and getting to know how they do daily life, why did I have such opposition to being like the culture here?"

> Ack! So exhausting. Contextualization! Ethnocentrism! Incarnational! Set-apart! Stop—stop, it hurts my head. I just wanna love on people. When did it get so complicated

---

[24] WEC International Contextualization Committee, "Guidelines for Contextualization" (Gerrards Cross, England: WEC International, 2009).

to tell someone about Jesus and give them a bowl of rice?
SF, Millennial Blog

The call for tolerance with which the younger generation has developed can create difficulty for them and for ministry leaders. Although many of them would say they have encountered God's love, resulting in deep and passionate worship, they wrestle with how to publicly apply personal convictions about truth and biblical teaching. These young Christians find themselves caught between modernity's unfounded confidence in rationality, science, and technology, and postmodernity's skepticism about any universal idea/truth, including the exclusive claims of Jesus and their implications. This generation abhors arrogance to the extent of struggling over how to demonstrate both humility and certainty. Although they may have a deep unshakable conviction about personal matters of faith, members of the younger generation also have a deep dread of appearing to "know it all."

> Being "tolerant" is highly regarded in our generation. It's frustrating that we seem to dilute "right" and "wrong" for the sake of tolerance to an unrecognizable point— like somehow it's a "one or the other" choice: be tolerant & loving or stand up for what you believe is good and true. Newsflash World: this black and white dichotomy is a bold-faced lie! I know there is much to be said for patience, listening, and acceptance. This is Jesus 101: he takes the broken and bloodied and makes them whole, welcomes them like children, accepts us as goofy misshapen children, but like any parent, he wants us to be whole, wants to teach us, hold our hands up as we climb the rocky slopes. If our parents decided to be "tolerant" of the way we were as toddlers, simply accepting our ignorance or disobedience—no sane parent would deem that loving. No! It would be cruel and negligent and the farthest from love: it really isn't love, this is chaos. *SF, Millennial Blog*

The postmodern ethos in which the Millennial is immersed arose in part as reaction to the rationalism and enlightened utopianism of modernity. Christianity centers existence and hope in thinking and willing as a reflection of the image of God. God meets with humanity in terms of human beings as temples of the Holy Spirit, called to know Him and fulfill His mission on earth.

Postmodernism asserts that human characteristics are simply the result of social, economic, and historic forces over which people have little or no control. Many young Christians agree and discount the modern myth of progress and certainty centered in humanity. While conceding that modernity has brought enormous benefits to human existence, postmoderns also see deficiencies. These include an arrogant intellectual elite that manages education and general thought; a science, supposedly empirical and objective, corrupted by special interests that pay for and benefit from results; and political structures used by leaders who advance their own causes and profit.[25]

Postmodern Christians are concerned that older evangelicals have failed to see the inherent weaknesses of modernity, with its confidence in science, technology, and reason providing the deep satisfaction humans crave. This results in the assumption that modernity is more biblically sound than postmodernity. The modern church's tendency to view all things postmodern in a negative light can result in failure to see any hope or positive opportunities for expressing the gospel within a worldview it rejects.

Millennials embrace diversity and plurality without the associated relativism. The biblically centered view they struggle to maintain is revolutionary, yet dates back to the Pauline desire to be "all things to all men" (1 Cor 9:22 NASB), always trying to see matters from the other's point of view. They expect to live with the benefits of science, medicine, and technology, but do not want to depend on them to meet the aspirations of the human heart as modernity might suggest. Finding a Christ-centered approach to postmodernism that is contextually appropriate and biblically faithful requires analyzing a range of resources that highlight the strengths and weaknesses of the youthful generation.

---

[25] Michael Pocock, Gailyn Van Rheenen, and Douglas McConnell, eds., *The Changing Face of World Missions: Engaging Contemporary Issues and Trends* (Grand Rapids: Baker Academic, 2005), 110.

GETTING READY TO GO

For seven years we led summer mission trips from a university church in Minneapolis to cities in Europe. Some members of these teams showed a strong desire to reach out to local people with the love and life of Jesus. Others were interested in touring, with a little ministry thrown in. We found that prefield preparation was critical to train everyone and to weed out those for whom the word "vacation" was the operative one in the phrase, "vacation with a purpose." This is one of the pitfalls of short-term missions. Although "a Princeton study found that 1.6 million people took short term trips—an average of eight days—in 2005," the research also showed that "vacation destinations are especially popular . . . the Bahamas receives one short-term missionary for every 15 residents."[26]

Then later there was the church group that arrived on one of our mission's West African fields. This short-term team had little prefield training and a casual connection with a national church leader in the country. When the group of teenagers arrived and deplaned, the national leader saw with horror the fifteen- to eighteen-year-old girls wearing "very immodest" (his words) shorts. In the USA, this apparel might have been accepted. In that African country, dressing this way made a statement about these girls they would have found appalling had they understood the culture. When they were asked to change their outfits, the teenagers were offended. In the end, the results were a disillusioned local church leader and congregation and a short-term

---

[26] Jacqueline L. Salmon, "Churches Retool Mission Trips," *Washington Post*, July 5, 2008, http://www.washingtonpost.com/wp-dyn/content/article/2008/07/04/AR2008070402233.html (accessed July 8, 2011).

group who thought "missions doesn't work." The importance of pre-field preparation and postfield debriefing cannot be overstated.

> Another mindset found in our culture is that of willing-ness to obey (to go into ministry) but very little emphasis on being prepared. *SF, Millennial Blog*

Mission trips offer a unique opportunity for mentoring and dis-cipling young people. With proper screening and training in place to make sure teens go for the right reasons, the short-term experience can be an excellent discipling tool. Ministering cross-culturally requires discipline, proactively engaging others, and personal holiness, all of which have appeal for the adventure-seeking, experience-oriented youth.

Short-term experiences can provide North American Christians with enlightening exposure to the world beyond the familiar and deepen understanding of missions and their own walk with God. Churches that send out short-term teams gain firsthand information and global awareness, and benefit from being actively and personally involved with missions. However, there is danger in the short-term strategy becoming an end in itself, resulting in neglect of long-term efforts, particularly in places where difficult language acquisition and cultural adaptation are necessary for communicating at heart level with local people. Missionary teams can benefit from the encourage-ment and creativity short-termers bring, but short-term ministry alone cannot fulfill the Great Commission. Continuity of ministry comes only from long-term commitment. Imagine any ministry in the USA surviving mainly on short-term, in-and-out efforts. Peter Wagner states that a key to growth in any church is the longevity of the pas-tor, allowing a trust/bond relationship to develop over years. Patrick Johnstone suggests that it takes, on average, seven years on a field be-fore a new missionary begins to function at more than a superficial level in preaching, discipling, and winning full acceptance.

When our daughter, Melanie, spent a year working in a boys' or-phanage in Beirut, the kids loved her, but there was always the sense that, like many others, she would soon leave and probably never see most of them again. Although a person can certainly touch lives in one year, effective mentoring and discipling takes much longer.

To touch the heart of a people and to see a church planted, workers must live in a culture long enough to gain insight into the culture's worldview and discover how to use that knowledge as a bridge for the gospel. The process of language and cultural adaptation, contextualization, and application of our message requires sensitivity, patience, and time as one of our former students working overseas explained:

> There is a dearth of workers (national or foreign) and resources to help. Since 1990 short-term workers have flocked to this country to work with Muslims in a free environment. Some good has been done, and some harm . . . The need, however, is for people who will stay for ten to twenty years, learn Turkish well, and live among the Millets and Turks. Those who do this gain credibility in ministry and provide a model in lifestyle.[27]

Millennial Christians are interested in seeing faith expressed in practice. Short-term mission trips fall into this category. Although initially disdained by seasoned missionaries, short-term experience is now generally recognized as a legitimate instrument for educating, mobilizing, and confirming a young person's interest in, and possible call to, missions. Short-term service can be a powerful introduction to the world and work of missions. However, it should not be the end, but only the beginning of lifelong interest in, and commitment to, God's work throughout His world. As Wendy Zoba concluded in her assessment of the value of short-term service, "It's too soon to tell if the mission-trip trend is raising a generation of disciples. But it's a start."[28]

---

[27] Evelyn Hibbert, *World Pulse*, 1995.

[28] Wendy Murray Zoba, "Youth Has Special Powers: The Millennial Generation May Be Uniquely Wired to Stand—and Sweat—for God," *Christianity Today*, February 5, 2001, http://www.ctlibrary.com/ct/2001/february5/10.56.html (accessed February 5, 2001).

> This is probably sacrilegious, err, forgive me, but short-
> term mission trips are like appetizers: once you taste the
> awesomeness of God working around the world you just
> want more. Your eyes are open to this vast need for Christ
> and it can change the course of your entire life. I know
> some people aren't big fans of the short-term mission trip,
> and I get it. It's expensive, it can feel like little to noth-
> ing of lasting impact was accomplished. Yet, if it weren't
> for the short-term mission trip I took in high school, I
> wouldn't have studied intercultural ministry at college nor
> be on my way to a life of cross-cultural mission. Just say-
> ing. *SF, Millennial Blog*

As assessment and training coordinators and then USA directors for WEC, questions about the young generation's willingness, attributes, and potential effectiveness were constantly in the forefront of our thinking. Would Millennials, coming out of the present cultural climate of North America, make successful missionaries / church workers? How prepared are these young people to yield to authority and experience? Are fears and apprehension in a world infiltrated by extremists undermining or strengthening their ministry resolve? What evangelism and discipleship models draw them and suit their abilities and inclinations? What are the most effective training and preparation methods for them? What organizational structures might need to be adjusted to more fruitfully accommodate these young people? How can organizations with a history of emphasizing proclamation ministry incorporate potential workers interested in community building and holistic ministry? How can mission organizations and churches gain new understanding and develop helpful strategies for recruiting and incorporating Millennials?

In preceding chapters we've taken a look at characteristics of the Millennial generation, the influence of postmodernism on its thought, and the still applicable commission Jesus gave to the church. Here we will consider how these directly connect in regard to missions/ministry.

Over the past twenty years, North American evangelical mission organizations have seen a significant decline in volunteers and financial resources. Dependent upon new recruits to keep the fulfillment of the Great Commission moving forward, missions seek connecting points between their goals and the ministry aspirations of potential new workers.

In 1997 the World Evangelical Fellowship commissioned a study to identify and define actual and perceived causes of missionary attrition.[29] A summary of the results disclosed the following characteristics that are vital for surviving life in ministry:

1. *Spirituality:* deep knowledge of and friendship with God, and awareness of His leading and calling.

2. *Relational Skills:* proud, demanding people weak in interpersonal skills generally fail on the mission field.

3. *Ministry Skills:* not necessarily achieved through formal education, and often honed in the local church. "There is absolutely no substitute for genuine, extensive, evaluated, pre-field ministry as an antidote to attrition."

4. *Training:* including, but not limited to, theological study. Specific field-related training including practical skills should be included.[30]

These skills and training are essential for successful workers of every generation. Eight years of responsibility for evaluating and assessing applicants' suitability for cross-cultural work in an international and interdenominational mission provided us with some insights into qualifications needed by missionary candidates. The list of character and training essentials found in the attrition study, as well as the reports of field workers, confirm our experience. The four categories provide us with reference points as we look at the younger generation and its potential for successful ministry.

---

[29] William David Taylor, ed., *Too Valuable to Lose: Exploring the Causes and Cures of Missionary Attrition*, World Evangelical Fellowship, Globalization of Mission Series (Pasadena: William Carey Library, 1997), xiv–xv.

[30] Ibid.

SPIRITUALITY

A hopeful sign for this generation and ministry is one of its labels: "Generation Give." Millennials feel a spiritual connection to suffering, often expressed in their voluntary responses to disasters like Hurricane Katrina in 2006 when thousands of college students poured into the Gulf states to help victims and clean up debris.

In addition to a willingness to serve others, personal spirituality seems to be on the rise in this generation. According to a *Time* magazine report, when Millennials began reaching college age in the late 1990s, enrollment at the USA's 104 "intentionally Christ-centered colleges" rose more than three times faster than enrollment at all four-year colleges. As one college senior told the magazine, "Young people want to know something bigger than themselves."[31]

Admittedly, spirituality for this generation may be superficial, representing little beyond a vague search for transcendence of the material world. There may be abandonment of the "religious practices" of faith that encourage character development and commitment, and an over-emphasis on friendship with God resulting in excessive reliance on intuition. Spirituality may represent dissatisfaction with the church that projects the image of a "club" with inside language and interests they don't understand or appreciate. Millennials are often simply uninterested in church or see the church as judgmental, although they're eager to talk about Jesus. They express disillusionment about the high value placed on profit, power, success, affluence, and personal peace by earlier generations of churchgoers.

It may also indicate a return to devotional piety or a new clique in the world of youth:

> In 1990 there were a few prayer circles or clubs in U.S. public high schools. Now there are over 10,000 of them, full of devout kids . . . Religion has become the basis of what the *LA Times* calls, "a new teenage social caste" that

---

[31] Rebecca Winters, "Higher Learning," *Time*, January 26, 2004, http://www.time.com/time/magazine/article/0,9171,582350,00.html (accessed August 19, 2009).

includes groups such as the Knights of Christ, who square off regularly against students who idolize antireligious rockers such as Marilyn Manson.[32]

The Christian polling agency led by George Barna notes that research shows two out of three teenagers strongly desire a personal relationship with God, even though fewer than half are excited about church. The question for church and mission leaders is how to reach this complicated and disparate group.[33]

Every generation has uniquely heard and responded to God's call. In North America we can look back at such events as the Great Awakening, the revivals of the nineteenth century, the Student Volunteer Movement beginning in 1886, and the Jesus Revolution of the 1970s. Each of these renewals of faith and dedication spurred Christians to plunge more zealously into spreading the gospel. Voices from within the Millennial generation itself are calling for their contemporaries to join them in God's purposes.

Claude Hickman, professional BMX stunt cyclist, heard about God's plan for the nations at a missions conference and worried that he might end up spending his life on things that didn't matter. Now a leader of The Traveling Team, a mission mobilizing organization, Hickman says to his peers: "He must have the freedom to interrupt our plans . . . Abraham heard God's voice telling him to go . . . to change his plans and join God in the journey."[34]

Ryan Shaw, a leader in SVM2—the current version of the Student Volunteer Movement[35]—compares the Millennial generation to a sleeping giant he believes can be awakened to appreciate and act on its privilege and responsibility to reach the unreached, and

---

[32] Strauss and Howe, *Generations*, 234.

[33] David Kinnaman, "Research on Youth and Spirituality," The Barna Group, http://www.barna.org (accessed December 23, 2009; article discontinued).

[34] Claude Hickman, *Live Life on Purpose: God's Purpose, Your Life, One Journey* (Eunumclaw, WA: WinePress, 2005), 57–58.

[35] Student Volunteer Movement 2, "Statement of Purpose," http://www.svm2.net (accessed May 23, 2008; page discontinued).

"to accomplish the Great Commission in our lifetime."[36] According to SVM2 research, however, critical problems in the North American church hinder the mission movement. These include a low standard of commitment to and promotion of long-term cross-cultural ministry among the unreached, poor cooperation in working together, lack of a unified prayer focus, lack of resources to help students launch mobilization initiatives among their peers, few connecting points between students and ministry leaders to network and share information and ideas, and lack of connectedness between spiritual revival and the church's effectiveness in carrying forward the Great Commission.

Todd Ahrend, one of the pioneers of The Traveling Team, believes every Christian should be a missions mobilizer, with a wealth of information and a growing spiritual passion to share with the young generation. He asks, "What if college students truly believed they could change the world? What if they truly had a passion for the lost? What if all the misconceptions of missions in the minds of people were gone?"[37]

The freshness and generational knowledge of these newer organizations and younger leaders can help more established ministries and leaders to be aware of the potential of Millennials and more sympathetic to their struggles and aspirations. The experience and knowledge of the older organizations and leaders can help Millennials to avoid pitfalls and learn to be more effective. It is human nature to think, "That's been said, or done, before. We've already tried that. Why reinvent the wheel? Just wait until they run up against the real problems. Oh, they're so young and inexperienced." Or, "They're such old dudes. They're stuck in tradition and the way things have always been done. Can't they see that we're about now? Don't they see that we're the ones who are going to change the world?" Those who follow Jesus need to communicate (which includes a lot of listening), inspire, and work

---

[36] Ryan Shaw, *Waking the Giant: The Resurging Student Mission Movement* (Pasadena: William Carey Library, 2006), 2.

[37] Todd Ahrend, "Overview: The Traveling Team," The Traveling Team, http://www.thetravelingteam.org/overview (accessed September 3, 2009; page discontinued).

together across the generations to fulfill His commission. Being learners is as vital in every other aspect of missions as it is in cross-cultural adaptation.

In the 1970s, as university students, we were part of a team from Minneapolis offered housing at WEC's headquarters outside London. We learned so much that became foundational to our faith and ministry lives during those years, but possibly nothing more important than the attitude we saw in the couple who were the international directors of the mission, Len and Iris Moules. After working in India and Tibet and leading the WEC British sending base, Len had become a well-known missionary statesman, speaker, and author who traveled the world. Yet what most impressed us brash young Americans was Len's way of looking for what we were learning and could share with him. He was the person we sought out when we faced a spiritual or practical issue we didn't know how to handle, and he would freely share with us wisdom gained through many years of sacrifice and blessing—but he treated us as if he were the "new" believer eager to absorb any truth or insight we had received. He was willing to go to the youngest missionary candidate for spiritual counsel. Len simply wanted "more of Jesus." What spiritual growth would take place, what helpful knowledge and counsel could be exchanged, what could be accomplished if everyone involved in the mission enterprise took this attitude?

RELATIONAL SKILLS

Millennials tend to see the "glory of God" rather than the "fear of hell" as motivation for service. Their faith is rooted in relationship more than creed. Their passion for worship and yearning to do something significant has given many of them a desire to live for Christ. Compared to previous generations, greater racial and cultural sensitivity as well as insatiable interest in cultural differences have positioned many of this group to effectively engage with cultures outside their own. They seem prepared to listen to people with other perspectives, which is a desirable characteristic for a successful missionary.

Generally, these young people operate with fewer racial stereotypes than their parents. They assume a person who speaks with negative racial overtones is ignorant. They tend to be quite willing to learn from those who do not look like them or have the same background, and indicate that they are willing to go overboard to communicate sensitivity and compassionate inclusion.

Millennials are idealistic about relationships, including interracial ones. Researchers Strauss and Howe argue that this generation has replaced the old agenda of racial discourse with a new agenda to "create opportunities for racial groups to shed their adult-imposed separateness."[38] One indication of the growing trend towards racial and cultural integration is that transracial marriages and multiracial children have become more common, with less attention paid to the cultural differences once associated with various races and ethnic groups. As the browning of America reaches critical mass, diverse Latin, Asian, African, and Arab elements will mix into an increasingly pureed "melting pot." The most recent data from UCLA's Higher Education Research Institute shows that interracial interaction among college freshmen has reached a record high.[39]

Most Millennials would say that discrimination in any form is both ignorant and unacceptable. Females expect to be regarded as equals and to have increasing opportunities in leadership, business, and academics. A heightened sense of inclusiveness is becoming normal in all spheres of activity. Anything less is considered distasteful. How deep these high ideals go, and how they are evidenced in everyday behavior, remain questions. For instance, our nineteen-year-old son invited a friend, who has Asperger's Syndrome and can be slightly awkward socially, to a Millennial church group activity. Afterwards, we were asked to not bring her again since the group found her "difficult." Millennials see themselves as much more tolerant, accepting, and open than older generations, but following through and putting their ideals into practice in real life can be weak.

[38] Strauss and Howe, *Generations*, 192.
[39] Ibid.

We are all about Jesus, we love Jesus, we love to love, we love loving the loveless and ugly, we are about justice for the poor, we are really concerned about how faith is expressed in daily life. We reject rejection. In general we want to champion the championless. Whoot, whoot! For those of us in Christ, we want to show the oppressed, the marginalized, that their salvation has come and is coming in Jesus—they need not prove themselves, they need not wear the right clothes or have the right job. They need not go to the "right" church or morph into some creepy version of the Cleavers. They are accepted because He accepts them. Jeepers! Not only that, but we care about their pain and want to do something about it. *SF, Millennial Blog*

Wouldn't we all agree those sentiments sound wonderful? But how would they play to our son's friend? She already knew plenty of rejection from her classmates. In one sad episode during high school, she joined the girls track team. Besides the usual cruel remarks and snubbing, when the girls were sent out on a distance run through town, the others took off and left her lost and bewildered. She ended up phoning her mother because she didn't know how to get back to the school. How tragic that her introduction to Christian peers ended the same way: they did not want her around.

Imagining that traveling overseas will make a young person able to reach across cultural and other barriers is similarly idealistic, but not realistic. One important way Millennials can prepare for cross-cultural work is by learning to interact with and value people who are different from themselves right here at home. The church should be taking the lead in this, rather than being a place where those who are "different" are not welcome.

Research has shown that loud, impatient, demanding people with weak interpersonal skills often fail on the mission field and in team situations. Millennials have been trained since childhood to respect and cooperate with others. Educators' organizations like the American Federation of Teachers have promoted "zero tolerance" for bullying, racial slurs, and fighting. Parents and teachers have discouraged socially inappropriate behavior. Whether this instruction has gone deeply into the hearts and minds of young people can be debated given the rising incidence of cyberbullying, but the effort is unrelenting.

Citizens and policymakers sometimes see the emphasis on zero tolerance as an overreaction to events. But as police officer Cliff Lauritzen states, "We may be overreacting, but if we don't, if we underreact and something happens, we had the opportunity and didn't take it."[40] Positively, the rate of school crime has dropped since "nearly every district notched up its rules, enforcements, and penalties. American schools are becoming no-nonsense places that—no surprise—are producing no-nonsense kids."[41] Sadly, bullying has not been eradicated. News reports of tragic consequences from bullying surface periodically.

Restrictions can be imposed on negative, inappropriate behavior, but ministry of the gospel in and through a community of believing people must go well beyond simply omitting unacceptable words and actions. Just being tolerant of others does not minister life-changing example and truth.

The younger generation appreciates change and usually sees change as improving society. They appreciate collaborating, a pattern established early in their learning cycle. In grade school they worked together on projects. As a professor, I frequently encourage joint efforts among students from making presentations to testing. At our college, faculty are encouraged to use "blended learning" including small-group discussions, Web-based instructional tools, and collaborative answers to questions. The students respond willingly and quickly to tasks where they meet together, formulate a plan, and complete an assignment. They are comfortable working together, typically with little concern about who is the leader or who is up front making the presentation.

Millennials often reflect a team mentality and actually seem to prefer working and learning in situations that include collaboration, group effort, and general rather than individual evaluation. They are usually willing to cooperate with their parents, whom they generally

---

[40] Ibid., 218.
[41] Ibid., 318.

respect; their grandparents, whom they admire; and those social insti-tutions that are viewed as supportive of their aspirations and concerned for their interests and well-being.

Appreciation for community life and cooperative alliances is dem-onstrated in a variety of ways by these young people, from loyalty to one another to the working style of companies like Zappos. Anyone familiar with this online shoe retailer is familiar with the informality and family atmosphere expressed in its ethos and customer contacts. Millennial values and attitudes play a large role in the company's strat-egy and work. Zappos is one of the most efficient online distributors in existence. Young workers want to be part of this type of business cul-ture. As Jane Buckingham writes: "Ads aimed at Gen Xers show them living solitary, miserable but interesting lives. That approach doesn't work with the next generation. Belonging to a group is so important that I caution anyone advertising to this generation against putting a lone individual in an ad."[42]

Millenials don't only want to appreciate and work closely with each other. They also admire and esteem older workers. Assuming that different generations will not work well together is a mistake. Given the younger generation's respect for the older, and the older genera-tion's fascination with the abilities—particularly with rapidly changing technology—and flexibility of the younger, effective cooperation can occur. Developing the relational skills of listening, accepting, appre-ciating the ideas and unique perspective of others, and being willing to adapt on personal preferences or cultural issues can all contribute to establishing ministry teams that are edifying and effective at home or abroad.

> The book has been thrown out! The old "rules" of minis-try, of the world, are in constant flux, and it's impossible to please everyone. I believe it's vital for inter-generational

---

[42] Jane Buckingham, "Ministry to Millennials: Understanding and Reaching the Next Generation," GCI Generations Ministries, http://genmin.wcg.org/ Webpercent20Documents/Millennials.pdf (accessed August 19, 2009; page discontinued).

ministry teams to be aware of the unique values they each possess. It's important to dialogue about this, bringing ideas and goals to scripture instead of tradition. We have grown up in a very different time from our predecessors, and miscommunication on the mission field can lead to much more than hurt feelings. *SF, Millennial Blog*

MINISTRY SKILLS TRAINING AND PREPARATION

For this generation, preparation and development of skills for ministry may begin with, but are not limited to, college. The sharpening of skills through service in a local church is often most helpful in gaining ministry experience and expertise.

By and large the young generation has tended to desire higher levels of education. Though they have more formal training than previous generations, they also face the missions-marginalizing issue of tremendous educational debt. More years in school can result in longer financial dependence on parents. A young person may continue living in the parental home after college, perhaps a wise financial plan, but something the older generations would have strenuously avoided. As might be expected, the CNA study mentioned previously reports that "more young people today are enrolled in college and have completed Bachelor's degrees or higher. The number of those who have attained only the level of a high school degree or less has declined since 1968."[43]

However, education for ministry extends beyond the classroom. Many friends who have attended seminary concur that upon leaving with a master of divinity degree, the challenge of learning to work together with others in a ministry setting commenced. New workers attempting to achieve the goals and ideals learned in class quickly recognize that real people do not simply line up neatly to fulfill ministry aspirations and strategies.

Millennials often recognize their need for assistance in dealing with difficult people or situations. Their tendency is to avoid confrontation, hoping problems will just go away. Members of every generation

---

[43] Stafford and Griffis, "Review of Millennial Characteristics."

demonstrate reluctance about confrontation, but today's young people absolutely abhor entering into disputes or strife with others. Their behavior can appear similar to those from Eastern cultures who put the highest priority on "saving face." No Millennial wants to embarrass or disrespect anyone else, and will go to great lengths and spend much time avoiding direct confrontation, even to the extent of dishonesty and/or leaving a problem to fester below the surface until it eventually explodes outward. They need to see trainers and fellow workers of the older generations facing up to difficulties, including dealing with people problems, from the perspective of what is right biblically and best for the team, with the goal of a positive result for all. Leaders should demonstrate that simply avoiding confrontation can lead to protracted and increasingly difficult confrontation in the future. Wise leaders will help aspiring young workers to discern when it is good to let issues play out to a quiet end and when this would be only "putting off the evil day" and lead to escalating problems.

The youthful generation anticipates that ministry training will be enjoyable, and they expect to be supported in the learning environment. They tend to think as "us" and appreciate cooperative learning and working, rather than independence and "turf wars."

As has been mentioned, an overly optimistic impression of the younger generation needs to be tempered with understanding of its tendency to inflate its abilities. Ardor at times borders on the impetuous and naïve. Employers and ministry organizations complain about overconfident and self-assured overestimation of skills and abilities. This can include unrealistic expectations of those who supervise them, especially for constant coaching and affirmation. Supervisors find these young folks to be high maintenance, but also to have the potential, when handled with care, to become capable workers.

This generation looks for supervision that includes precise feedback. Supervisors are sometimes surprised by parents' heavy involvement in their children's assessment, even calling to question their children's evaluations. Constant engagement and communication regarding the level of feedback desired is more effective than proceeding based on the norms of previous generations' expectations. In addition young people desire more than good feelings in training, work, or ministry. They want to be engaged in activity that produces tangible results. Anything deemed "busy work," with no explanation of its purpose or goal, results in a disgruntled young worker.

> I don't think Millennials hate menial tasks, we just hate them when we have to do them by ourselves with no apparent purpose—it's much easier when we as a team clean up a neighborhood or fold a bunch of support letters. It's much more fun when you're not alone—I think this is demonstrated really well in short-term missions. *SF, Millennial Blog*

One of the most popular vocational training and preparation options for the younger generations is the internship. To be successful, in the young person's mind, the internship should include preparatory orientation and training, a clear purpose for internship activities, guidance and structure, and intentional balancing of what might be perceived as mundane with duties of substance and value to both the organization and the intern. Discussions of how the intern is doing must take place frequently, not exclusively at the conclusion of the program. The millennial appreciates this exercise being carried out as informally as possible, with the supervisor possibly looking for individuals during a break or a meal and engaging in talking over their opinions of the internship, what they are learning, etc. Promoting a relaxed, caring mentor relationship will achieve good results in the long term.

Another invaluable training tool is study abroad. Where there may be fear, misunderstanding, and cultural misattribution, nothing else is a true substitute for firsthand knowledge of another culture. Spending time getting to know people from other backgrounds and learning to live in their environment generally opens a world of appreciation and empathy.

Because so much of the world's population lives outside our borders and, increasingly, many ethnic groups are moving inside our borders, study and experience of different cultures is vital. Our young people here and abroad need to know how to engage the world. Short-term mission trips may provide a taste of another culture, but living and studying inside that culture for a year or more takes students beyond the surface in relationships and understanding.

Training and preparation for ministry must take place on three levels: academic, practical, and spiritual. One young missionary's story demonstrates the critical necessity for building a strong biblical, theological, missiological, and spiritual foundation for serving overseas. After being immersed for several years in a culture antagonistic to Christianity, she began to doubt the exclusive claims of Christ. As a student in the USA, she had completed required Bible courses and done well academically, but under the pressures of an environment hostile to her faith, she realized much of her knowledge was purely cerebral and had not taken hold in the deepest parts of her being. She had attended classes on the person and work of Christ, listened to lectures, and gotten good grades, but that was insufficient for ministry. After a furlough that included counseling and reexamination of the basic tenets of the faith, together with periods of retreat, prayer, and personal ministry, she was able to return to her field of service with renewed confidence in her faith, satisfied that it is true both academically and experientially.

In addition to their propensity for increased education, many of the younger generation have joined a growing spiritual movement toward the contemplative. Mark Yaconelli, of the Youth Ministry and Spirituality Project, states:

> I don't believe ancient disciplines and contemplative practices of the church will ever be as widespread and popular as game nights, ski retreats, and those models of ministry that imitate the surrounding culture. But in the next ten to twenty years, more youth workers will recognize that, in this period of the life of the church, it's silence that proclaims the good news, stillness that brings justice, fasting

that feeds the hungry, and prayer that trains the heart to
hear the quiet beckoning of the living Christ.[44]

Though arguably often neglected activities in churches major-
ing on worship, speakers, and facilities that are more seeker friendly,
learning to be still before the Lord and to converse with Him are in-
dispensable spiritual skills for people contemplating cross-cultural
ministry. Mentoring in these spiritual disciplines is possibly the most
important part of preparation for missionary service. Without such
vital personal connection with God, a worker won't survive spiritually.

Today's educated young adults live in a world they perceive as having few boundaries or borders. Most of them hold a global, multiethnic,
multicultural view of the world. Due to its use of technology, this generation assumes it understands the world. Confidence results in high
mobility as many of them move easily between cultures and are willing
to consider varied vocational and ministry options. Their preference for
making incremental decisions based on affirmation, a sense of belonging, and keeping their options open, can cause tension for leaders and
organizations who value long-term commitment.

All generations show strengths and weaknesses, and today's generation is no exception. They are adept at multitasking and completing
large tasks well at the last minute. They are not cowed by authority,
although they respect the experience of older generations. They will
move on to different work opportunities as they discover how they
are "wired" or if they feel undervalued. They demand "the immediate
gratification of making an immediate impact by doing meaningful
work immediately."[45] As employees, or members of a ministry organization, supervisors find them to be high-maintenance, high-risk,
and—often—high-output workers.

---

[44] Mark Yaconelli, "Seven Trends to Watch in the Next Decade," Youth Specialties,
http://www.youthspecialties.com/freeresources/articles/culture/seven.php (accessed
August 2, 2009; page discontinued).

[45] Jim Heskett, "How Will Millennials Manage?," Harvard Business School,
August 2, 2007, http://hbswk.hbs.edu/item/5736.html (accessed December 24,
2009).

CHAPTER FIVE

IS FEAR A FACTOR?

The media urges us all to aim for the "American dream," with 2.3 perfect children, a comfortable home in the suburbs, up-to-date vehicles and electronic devices, a fulfilling career, and a secure retirement. Why would anyone choose to leave behind the amenities and prosperity of life in North America for the uncertainties, discomforts, and dangers of cross-cultural work?

I (Jim) understand the tendency to subside into this lifestyle without ever questioning whether it might be God's calling to live another way. I have also encountered the kinds of fears and hesitations a person may face in considering whether to answer God's call to cross-cultural work.

While living and working in California, I struggled because I believed God might want our family to go back into missions. But I was satisfied with our pleasant life. Even more, I found myself gripped with fear about leaving my job and accompanying benefits, including full health care, when one of our children suffered from severe asthma.

"I think I need to go to the doctor," little David would say in quiet, sad tones reflecting his first five years of life with serious asthma: often being rushed to the hospital at midnight gasping and wheezing; innumerable needles, medications, and breathing treatments; a child's intense fear of impending pain battling an experienced patient's knowledge that he required medical help.

Despite our best efforts at following medication protocols for David's asthma condition, every month meant many clinic visits and usually at least one frightening and draining trip to the emergency department where we had to help hold him down as he sobbed,

"No more shots! No more shots!" while the doctors injected epinephrine again and again.

We wondered about David's health in light of our family's future. After thirteen years working with a church-based, tent-making mission organization in the capital cities of Europe, we had taken a break at home in the USA. Jim had found a reasonably well-paying job that provided good medical benefits, and we were renting a comfortable apartment in a southern California beach town.

But at every turn we seemed to bump into missionaries, receive a greeting card with WEC applications enclosed, or hear a missions speaker at church. We knew we were not prepared to walk away from our call to global missions. While in Europe, we had lived at WEC's main base in England, renting extra space on the Bulstrode estate that no one thought would ever be needed for the mission's use! We'd heard many stories about God faithfully meeting needs in finances, family, and ministry. We were always fascinated but thought tent making suited us better. Though convinced the stories of God's deliverance were real, and having seen God miraculously meet major needs at the headquarters, we still thought the "life of faith" must be a privileged experience for certain missionary saints.

Eventually we realized God was leading us into WEC, along the lines of Norman Grubb's words: "Once Caught, No Escape." We gave in and became willing to pursue this direction from the Lord. We began to grow in confidence that God could provide not only for the giants of the faith but for our own family as well. We took steps to join WEC, and saw the Lord bless us with a financial gift that would launch us out into a new world of uncertainty and adventure.

Just as we were preparing to leave for candidate orientation in Pennsylvania, fears about David's health bubbled up. Were we irresponsible to take David away from the medical resources he seemed to need so desperately? Well-meaning Christian friends reinforced these fears by voicing their concerns:

What about the medical coverage you have through your job? How will you pay for medication and treatment?

Why would you leave the doctors who know your son?

Does it make sense to go overseas, where there may be health risks and minimal medical care, with three young children (one who is chronically ill)?

When Jim prayed about this, asking the Lord to confirm His leading to us by healing David, we saw no answer. In fact, just two weeks before we were scheduled to leave California for Pennsylvania, David had an asthma attack severe enough to force us to the local emergency room. Jim says, "I wish I could testify to being a man of faith and power, but as we drove east across the country to the WEC center, I did so with much fear and trembling." We knew God was asking us to take this step into missionary service, but we did not know where we would end up working or how David's medical needs would be taken care of.

Following our move to Pennsylvania, David never had another asthma attack that required a visit to the doctor or a trip to the hospital. Did the Lord heal him? Or did He know the environments where He would take us over the next twenty years, including Tasmania, Australia, and Vancouver, Canada, would be more conducive to David's healthy breathing? All we know is that David has not suffered from severe asthma since we set off for candidate training. The Lord knew we needed His encouragement in the early days of our adventure of faith and His confirmation that "your family is safest in the center of God's will."

Like us, in addition to their own hesitation about leaving the comforts and provisions of life at home, today's young Christians sometimes find their fears substantiated by well-intentioned parents, pastors, and friends who worry about the dangers of ministry outside North America. Many are discouraged from even considering cross-cultural ministry by the anxieties of those who influence them and consciously or subconsciously communicate fear of other countries and religions. When she said she was thinking about future ministry among people considered dangerous, one of my students was told, "You're going there? You're going to die!" Parents who continually hover about to rescue their children from any difficulty affect their children's outlook on life and therefore on ministry. The result can be grown-up children who are unduly influenced by significant elders to believe working among people who are "different from us" is too dangerous.

C. T. Studd, the founder of WEC, never sat in a comfortable office in London directing the mission. He went off to Africa at the age of fifty-two, in poor health, and poured himself into evangelism, translation, and church leadership in uncomfortable and even dangerous surroundings until his death. He never asked those who followed him into WEC to do what he was not already doing.

As leaders of the WEC USA sending base, we were often contacted by parents who were believers but worried about their children heading for mission work abroad. Questions like "How are you going to guarantee her safety?" "Why does he have to go to a dangerous place like . . .? "There is so much need here, why should my child go overseas where who knows what could happen?" were common.

We would try to patiently explain that their (adult) children were answering the call of God for their lives, that there is no place in this world where safety can be guaranteed, and that truly the safest place for anyone to be is where God wants him or her in His plan. While reassuring them that every reasonable health and safety precaution would be taken, we explained that cross-cultural work does involve risks a person might avoid by staying home. Their children, aware of this, had still chosen to obey God's call.

This was all well and good until the day *our* daughter, Melanie, a university student, announced that she wanted to join WEC short term to serve for a year in a boys' orphanage in Beirut, Lebanon. To our generation of Americans, Beirut is a synonym for chaos, based on news images of piles of rubble and figures waving automatic weapons at stopped vehicles. In fact, we had sometimes told Melanie to clean up her room, saying, "It looks like Beirut in here." At the time, Lebanon was hit regularly by Israeli rockets, and Syrian soldiers with machine guns patrolled the streets.

Reassuring reluctant parents about their child's decision is one thing; seeing your own daughter choose to work in a war zone is quite another. I (Judy) remembered years earlier talking with my own mother about the privilege God was giving her when both my sister and I, with my husband and small children, headed overseas. Thinking about how the Lord holds us to our words, I had to remind myself that the same faithful God who called and led us, was calling and leading Melanie—and giving us the privilege of releasing our child for His service.

Jim had an even tougher time than I, partly because Melanie is the only daughter among our seven children, and also because he had experienced war firsthand and could not only imagine rocket attacks, but remembered what they were like. We gained new understanding and patience toward the parents who expressed their misgivings and fears to us.

In the end we knew God was leading Melanie to Beirut, and we knew that we must do what we encouraged others to do. Jim was able to visit Melanie in Lebanon, and though he found the constant presence of armed soldiers a bit disconcerting, he was encouraged by what God was doing in the lives of the boys at the orphanage and in Melanie's life. He saw that even nights spent in a bomb shelter helping the littlest boys recite Bible verses about God's care and protection, singing, and praying, were being used as God's tools to bring them closer to Him.

Melanie experienced life as it is lived by so many people, including our fellow Christians, in insecure areas throughout the world. She learned that even as rockets exploded, God was faithful and present and speaking to her of His love and care. Her walk with Him took on new depth. She forged friendships that continue despite distance, separation, and cultural differences, and grew tremendously—emotionally, mentally and spiritually. And her parents were reminded yet again: the "safest" and best place for any of us is not determined by geography or governmental stability but by God's plan.

Apart from the worries of parents and others, both our experience and survey data reinforce the opinion that a combination of apprehension and lack of understanding about cross-cultural situations has great impact upon the decision-making process of Millennials. A number of events propel this fear, none more compellingly than the events of 9/11: "Their catalyzing generational event—the one that binds them as a generation, the catastrophic moment they all witnessed during their first, most formative years—is, of course, the terrorist attacks on September 11, 2001."[46] Historians and those who study generational differences agree that the attack on the World Trade Center was traumatic for, and left an emotional imprint on, all living generations. The emotional response differed from individual to individual, but for the younger generations this event and its aftermath, the ongoing war on terror, have affected how they understand themselves as future adults, parents, and global citizens.

A decade after 9/11, emotional reactions have settled somewhat, and workers have returned to many of the ministry locations they had left. However, a residue of fear remains below the surface for many, especially Americans. In an interview for *Christianity Today*, mission strategist Patrick Johnstone was asked, "You have said elsewhere that September 11 may greatly reduce what you call 'Christian tourism' or the high number of short-term mission trips offered through North American churches and mission agencies. Do you still think so?"

Johnstone responded:

> The point for Christians is that it's now not just a simple matter of, "Oh, I'll go to that country for a visit." You've got to seriously consider whether to go, because there is an element of danger. This is going to lead to a much more

---

[46] Claire Raines, "Managing Millennials," Claire Raines Associates, http://www.generationsatwork.com/articles/millenials.html (accessed September 13, 2009 (page discontinued).

serious contemplation about traveling overseas, especially in countries where there's a significant Islamic presence.[47]

Mission leaders are concerned because present Christian outreach to strongly Muslim areas of the world makes up only two percent of the total mission effort. Because of the challenges to sharing the gospel and the slow response rate in these places, missions have often followed the strategy of applying resources and personnel to places that are less resistant. Islam's recent expansion is daunting. Muslims now make up Switzerland's third largest religious community, after Protestants and Catholics. At its present rate of growth, Islam will be the largest religious community, as well as the largest population group, in the country in less than twenty years. Given Switzerland's strong Christian history, this is an astounding trend.

Patrick Johnston writes: "Muslims see the conversion of England to Islam as a key strategy for winning Europe."[48] Samuel P. Huntington contends that although Christianity has been the fastest growing religion in the world by conversion (not biological) growth, "the relative share of global population will fall steeply in the new century, and this religion has been supplanted by Islam. In the long run Muhammad wins out."[49] Islam's claim to be the perfect and final revelation of the one true religion that supersedes Judaism and Christianity presents us with a formidable challenge. Will Millennial Christians, entering the work and ministry force today and tomorrow, accept this challenge or be held back by fear and other factors?

The prohibition of traditional Christian missionary activity requires use of creative, intentional strategies for entering and remaining in most Islamic nations. The need for constant attention to security, especially in communications, emphasizes the risks of moving into these

---

[47] Patrick Johnstone, "September 11 Prompts Sober Missions Thinking," *Christianity Today*, August 2002, http://www.christianitytoday.com/ct/2002/augustweb-only/8-26-51.0.html (accessed June 28, 2008).

[48] Patrick J. Johnstone, *Operation World*, 21st Century ed. (Waynesboro, GA: Paternoster, 2001), 654.

[49] Samuel P. Huntington, *The Clash of Civilizations and the Remaking of World Order* (New York: Simon & Schuster, 1996), 65.

environments. Hearing about violation of human rights and persecution of Muslim-background believers may put off Millennials, who are unfamiliar with life in a culture where becoming a follower of Jesus can be dangerous. News reports on the burning of churches in India or the death sentence for a pastor in Iran who refused to recant his Christian faith are unsettling. Misunderstanding about the "violent" nature of Islam, assuming most Muslims are hostile and favor violent jihad, creates fear and avoidance among Christians. "Islamophobia" is a term coined to describe prejudice towards and fear of Muslims. A recent *Washington Post / ABC News* poll found that 33 percent of Americans believe Islam encourages violence against non-Muslims, 46 percent have unfavorable attitudes towards Islam, and 58 percent say there are more violent extremists within Islam than in other religions.

As an example of the anti-Muslim propaganda making the rounds of the Internet, the following "quiz" was forwarded to our email by a friend:

Subject: Profiling Test

In 1972 at the Munich Olympics, athletes were kidnapped and massacred by
a. Olga Corbett
b. Sitting Bull
c. Arnold Schwarzenegger
d. Muslim male extremists between the ages of 17 and 40

In 1983 the U.S. Marine barracks in Beirut were blown up by
a. A pizza delivery boy
b. Pee Wee Herman
c. Geraldo Rivera
d. Muslim male extremists between the ages of 17 and 40

In 1993 the World Trade Center was bombed the first time by
a. Richard Simmons
b. Grandma Moses
c. Michael Jordan
d. Muslim male extremists between the ages of 17 and 40

On 9/11/01, four airliners were hijacked: two were used as missiles to take out the World Trade Center towers; one crashed into

the Pentagon; and one was diverted and crashed by its passengers. Thousands of people were killed that day by
a. Bugs Bunny, Wiley E. Coyote, Daffy Duck, and Elmer Fudd
b. The Supreme Court of Florida
c. Mr. Bean
d. Muslim male extremists between the ages of 17 and 40

In June 1968, Bobby Kennedy was murdered by
a. Superman
b. Jay Leno
c. Harry Potter
d. Muslim male extremist between the ages of 17 and 40

The complete mock quiz included another ten questions, all with the same "correct" answer. The ignorance and irrationality of its author are exemplified by the fact that Bobby Kennedy's assassin is a Christian Palestinian. However, the implication, probably unquestioned by many recipients of this email, is that Muslims should be feared, hated, and marginalized. Innumerable similar examples circulate daily via the World Wide Web. News reports and talk shows prey on the public's insecurities by emphasizing what terrorists (read "Islamic extremists") may do next. The unanimous verdict by watchdog groups like the European Monitoring Center on Racism and Xenophobia is that the Western media stirs up fear and prejudice towards Islam and reinforces the image of Islam as the enemy.

Subsequent to the 9/11 attacks, we were invited to a seminar at the State Department in Washington, DC. The officials there provided information and security suggestions to leaders of mission organizations with workers overseas. While recognizing that missionaries can indeed become "soft targets" in some countries, they emphasized that terrorist groups make up an extremely small percentage of any population, and that the majority in every area seek to live peacefully.

While visiting the Middle East, I heard many Muslim leaders express their embarrassment at the conduct of violent, self-appointed Islamic jihadists. When I asked why more of them did not speak up against the violence, they stated that most are fearful of repercussions.

They recognize that if they speak out, the terrorists' guns are turned on them.

In Islamic areas, those who respond to the Christian message may find the guns aimed at them as well. Converts may be rejected by their families and communities, be barred from an education, lose their jobs, and even face prison or death. Young people considering ministry in restrictive areas of the world must come to grips with the possible implications for those who respond positively to the gospel.

To further investigate feelings and attitudes affecting Millennials' decisions about engaging in cross-cultural work, we surveyed 251 college students and young adults. The questionnaire addressed experience living outside the USA; knowledge of other people groups, specifically Muslims; attitudes; experience with Muslims in friend/acquaintance relationships; concern for safety if called to live and minister in a Muslim context; and current evangelism activities. Results can be generalized as follows:

1. Few respondents have taken steps to get to know people of other cultural/ethnic backgrounds. Assumptions trumped personal, experiential knowledge.

2. As expected, people with little knowledge of other cultures had the greatest reluctance to reach out for friendship or ministry purposes. Those who had more personal knowledge of other cultures (i.e., overseas experience, etc.) were more comfortable reaching out for cross-cultural friendships as a normal part of life. Lack of knowledge about cultural/religious differences, coupled with fear of miscommunication or misunderstanding, paralyzed would-be cross-cultural contact.

3. Increased experiential knowledge of other ethnicities resulted in a much more positive attitude towards them, especially regarding issues like extremism and illegal entry to the USA, confirming Martin Luther King Jr.'s comment, "Men often hate each other because they fear each other; they fear each other because they don't know each other; they don't know each other

because they cannot communicate; they cannot communicate because they are separated."[50]

One young lady explained that, after she returned from a short-term mission in the Middle East, she was appalled by the ignorance and caricatures Americans held about the people she had spent a year getting to know and appreciate. Arguments developed and frustrations arose as she realized she was not able to meaningfully communicate the incredible hospitality and friendliness she had discovered in a nation many of her friends feared.

Generations differ in the way they view people who are culturally or ethnically different from them. When asked, "What is your first thought when you hear the word 'Muslim'?" the majority of our contemporaries answered, "Terrorist."

Asked the same question in the survey, the largest number of Millennials responded "devoutly religious" or "blind and misguided." Interestingly, the word "terrorist" was completely absent. Only 8 percent mentioned anything relating to violence or hostility.

During personal interviews conducted with a smaller number of students in conjunction with the survey, those who had spent significant time outside North America seemed uncomfortable discussing questions like, "What percent of American Muslims are illegal immigrants?" Generally, today's young people, educated in liberal arts settings and impatient with cultural stereotypes, tend to be tolerant, respectful, and accepting of all religions, and wary of using "politically incorrect" terminology.

Although they would not embrace Islamic doctrine and practice as truth, Christian Millennials are clearly hesitant to appear bigoted in any way towards Muslims. Their experience of other cultures may be limited, but the present mindset of sensitivity towards differences seems to make them particularly reticent to appear judgmental. A number of respondents commented about "not wanting to judge them," "not wanting to assume bad things about them," and "I can't

---

[50] Martin Luther King Jr., *Stride toward Freedom: The Montgomery Story Papers* (New York: Harper, 1958), 188.

make assumptions about them." This lines up with the survey, where the majority stated that they do not know any Muslims well enough to have specific attitudes about them. Only a small percentage (15 percent) gave negative comments centered on "their beliefs," "they hate Americans," "because of 9/11," or "because of the extremists."

Most of those interviewed did not feel the majority of Muslims actively engage in or support violent jihad against the West. A number said they would be willing to go to minister among Muslims, but highlighted the necessity of having a specific or "special" calling, not just an inclination, to do so. Responses as to levels of concern about danger were mixed. Some expressed appreciation for the Islamic community lifestyle. A significant portion felt their generation is strong in willingness to "strip ourselves of our nationalism and our patriotism, our tendency to defend and even embrace American views and policies."

In spite of this sentiment, the interviews revealed that few had much knowledge of or experience with people who were not like them. Some students did comment on the value of short-term trips as an educational/experiential resource for future ministry.

Interviews were carried out by student volunteers in hope that the interviewees would share freely with a peer rather than tailoring their responses to fit what an authority figure might want to hear, and concentrated on attitudes toward ministry in Muslim contexts. Particularly interesting excerpts from some of these interviews include:

> One of my interviewees had serious questions about his willingness to go, or especially about going with a wife (he just recently got engaged). He was convinced that he would not be willing to take his wife into this kind of ministry. Another concluded that he would not be well suited for this kind of intense ministry.

> Personally I would approach Muslim missions with a mixture of fear and excitement. I love Muslim culture, but to be honest, sometimes Muslims frighten me. Perhaps it is because of the way they have been linked to terrorism, and perhaps it is the way the Muslims have persecuted

Christians, but I find myself "walking on eggshells" around them as though saying the wrong thing might start an argument.

I believe fear of Muslims is one of the largest barriers within our generation. I think fear is the main issue that people considering ministry to Muslims are facing. In fact, all of the individuals I surveyed said, "Fear" as their first reaction if God called them to ministry among Muslims. This fear stems from what they know about Islam being a highly strict, even oppressive, religion.

There has been a pushback on calls for "sacrifice," perhaps because of abuses of authority and power, but in my mind also because our generation is increasingly resistant towards anything that doesn't put me and my best interest (as determined by the world's standard of health, wealth, and happiness) at the forefront. We want the easy, painless road, the one requiring the least amount of sacrifice.

I rather like being a free woman in American society, and I would find it difficult to adjust to the restrictions placed on me in some Islamic cultures.

I am concerned that much of the enthusiasm or openness to go (to difficult countries) consists of, "Gee, that's a great idea," but not, "Gee, that's a great idea for me."

Millennials are not deterred by the thought of dying for the sake of Christ, but it appears to be much more difficult for them to give up a comfortable, wealthy life for the sake of Christ.

Millennials do not fear being killed for their faith; rather they fear going into a mission field that has been historically unfruitful. It would be hard to keep supporters because there may not be rapid converts.

The idea that potential missionaries of the next generation express no fear of death for their beliefs is an intriguing one. Although studies of martyrdom demonstrate that more people are dying for their faith in Christ today than in the first century, few contemporary American

Christians have experienced any sort of religious persecution or know someone who has. The interviewees all acknowledged that their sentiments about persecution originate exclusively from secondhand accounts they have read, heard, or seen in films. They have little personal experience of pressure or loss due to being Christians.

For believers in many other nations, persecution is a common experience, not an aberration. On a visit to Malaysia I met pastors who live in the midst of a Muslim majority and was awed to see how for them it was business as usual to minister under the constant threat of imprisonment. These Malaysian Christians were a reminder of what Jesus told his disciples would certainly be their experience:

> If the world hates you, you know that *it hated* Me before it hated you. If you were of the world, the world would love its own. Yet because you are not of the world, but I chose you out of the world, therefore the world hates you. Remember the word that I said to you, "A servant is not greater than his master." If they persecuted Me, they will also persecute you . . . All these things they will do to you for My name's sake, because they do not know Him who sent Me. (John 15:18–21 NKJV)

Has freedom from persecution and serious challenges to faith weakened the resolve of the American church and its ability to endure physical and/or emotional assault or oppression? Ryan Shaw, leader of the Student Volunteer Movement 2, posed this question:

> Might this hinder the church greatly from being effective in these kinds of global and political situations? Don't hear me saying America's mission days are over. I in no way subscribe to this, but I do believe we have to teach and prepare our young people much differently than they are being taught and prepared currently in the church. We need a massive shift. I spoke with Paul Borthwick along these lines recently, asking him what he thought some new paradigms for discipleship in America need to be to deal with these issues. His response as he chuckled was, "Is I

don't have a clue a sufficient answer?" His point was well taken, yet it does need to be considered.[51]

And we might well ask along with a 2009 *EMQ* article:

Is the world today really more dangerous for missionaries than it was for those early pioneers who answered the missions call? Consider the toll taken by disease, the dangers of travel on less-than-seaworthy vessels, the hostility of other faiths against the Christian witness and colonial governments more interested in commerce than spreading the gospel. Is the danger really greater today? Perhaps it is time for the Church in the West to turn its attention to a theology of suffering.[52]

A survey of approximately four hundred churchgoers and Christian Millennials completed for my doctoral dissertation compared the attitudes toward Muslims held by different generations. Note the descriptions of Muslims by generations other than Millennials, and then the descriptions by Millennials:

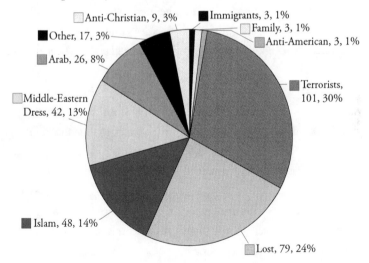

Multigenerational Responses to Muslims

---

[51] Ryan Shaw, email message to authors, April 17, 2008.

[52] Philip Thornton and Jeremy Thornton, "Why They Don't Go: Surveying the Next Generation of Mission Workers," *Evangelical Missions Quarterly* (April 2008).

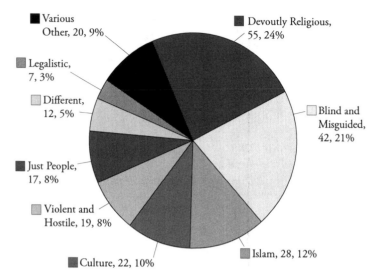

Millennial Attitude to Muslims

Obviously the older generations see Muslims differently, and that difference is associated in most cases with fear and distance. Whether the dangers are real, imagined, or exaggerated, those of us who have grown up in unparalleled comfort and safety must deal with what Jesus' instruction to take up the cross and follow Him means for us in regard to missions.

One of the students interviewed commented, "Fear of persecution has never been a huge fear of mine. In a strange, eerie way I've always felt like the Lord is preparing me for something like that to come." According to research, this is not typical of the majority of Millennials. Most of them seem to have little real awareness of what it is like to live outside the protective bubble of life in North America or without easy access to every form of technology and comfort. They need significant instruction and mentoring from mature believers to help them understand that sacrifice does not always refer to death for faith, but more often to releasing the sense of security and the lifestyle they see as necessary to their existence.

Confidence to follow the Lord into ministry in potentially dangerous situations flows from establishing confidence in your own ultimate future. No amount of the power of positive thinking or the promise of safety in all circumstances (which cannot be guaranteed anyway) can produce the ability to function effectively in stressful, risk-filled situations.

As a new Christian, serving in Vietnam as a combat platoon leader, I discovered that peace of mind and resolve to function came only on a deep faith level. What was my ultimate identity? What if I died, as had been the experience of fellow soldiers and officers? Was death the worst that could happen? How can a person who follows Jesus go confidently wherever he or she is sent? Only by total trust in His goodness, and by willingness even to die for the One who is worthy of such a sacrifice, can peace be attained when faced with death.

A critical element for this young generation—or anyone—choosing to work cross-culturally is hearing and responding to a call to yield unreservedly to the Lord Jesus. For Millennials, the call to surrender themselves to Him seems to be more compelling than the need to reach specific mission goals. Biblical passages such as "Don't you realize that your body is the temple of the Holy Spirit, who lives in you and was given to you by God? You do not belong to yourself" (1 Cor 6:19 NLT) are pivotal. Exhortation to change geographical location in response to the needs of the world and unreached people groups, while important, does not appear to be the essential feature in their choice of cross-cultural ministry. Rather, a call to surrender to Jesus and His plans for them as a declaration of love and worship seems to be catalytic in their lives.

As one of our interviewees explained, "I went to a youth conference down in Atlanta, Georgia . . . Throughout that week, through speakers, through fellowship, through all that we did I think the Lord just really woke me up. I was holding back and had a lot of things I was compromising on and had a lot of bad habits. And so, I just had to say at that conference that if I'm going to follow Jesus I have got to give everything."

These young people seem to unite around and be captivated by a call to embrace God's mission for them personally, rather than allying themselves to an organization's plans and objectives. They attach themselves to people they connect with and whose heart for ministry resonates with their own. Instead of acting out of loyalty to an organization, they are more willing to yield their personal plans for a greater cause when enticed by an ethos such as this:

> The transcendent message of God's sure triumph gives us the necessary distance and sobriety in respect to this world as well as the motivation to involve ourselves in the transformation of the status quo. Precisely the vision of God's triumph makes it impossible to look for sanctuary in quietism, neutrality, or withdrawal from the field of action.[53]

Each student interviewed recognized the potential danger of cross-cultural ministry and expressed willingness to accept the implications, indicating that a call to sacrifice could be met with enthusiastic affirmation by a young audience when coupled with the biblical claim to every part of life. One of them said,

> I think about the danger of working among peoples different than I grew up with, and my mother worries about it. However, I remind myself that my life is not my own. My heart overflows like a cup whenever I hear the gospel being preached to nonbelievers. I love the stories about how God is revealing Himself to other nations.

Most of these same students indicated struggling if their parents were not supportive of their plans to enter cross-cultural ministry in threatening places. Yet it does not appear that the hesitation about their parents' feelings always caused turning back from a sense of calling or leading from the Lord. As one interviewee explained,

> Honestly, it makes me sad when my mom worries over me or wishes I wouldn't risk my life. When she tells me that she worries, I feel that she doesn't understand how important it is to be willing to sacrifice your conveniences for God's call. I know that she is loving and operating

---

[53] Bosch, *Transforming Mission*, 510.

from a practical mindset, but it hurts to think she doesn't wholeheartedly encourage me.

Fresh approaches to the biblical call to sacrifice and willingness to lay down even life itself are needed as mission mobilizers continue to press this rallying cry to service. Jesus' own life and teaching model the admonition from John 15:13, "Greater love has no one than this: to lay down one's life for one's friends." The early church saw many examples of sacrificial commitment, from Stephen's stoning at the feet of Saul to the martyrs in the Roman Coliseum.

Believers need to hear about those who throughout history have faced death with resolute commitment to Jesus. Stories need to be told of people like Perpetua, Saturas, and Felicitas, North African Christians martyred in 202 AD. During their stay in prison, they continually told others about their faith. The day before their scheduled deaths, as they ate their last meal, a crowd gathered outside the cell. The believers spoke to the crowd with their usual courage, speaking of God's judgment of those who refuse Him and of their own happiness at giving their lives for His kingdom. Saturus said, "Note our faces well, that you may recognize us on the Day of Judgment." The observers were surprised at such peace and joy in the face of death. Later many became believers themselves.[54]

Mission history is full of the stories of those who have lived and died to spread God's truth around the globe. We have both found great encouragement and a spur to action in the lives of people like Hudson Taylor, Jonathan and Rosalind Goforth, C. T. and Priscilla Studd, Amy Carmichael, Norman Grubb, Helen Roseveare, and George Verwer. Reading or hearing the stories of missionary and local believers martyred in China, Korea, the Congo, the Amazon, Papua New Guinea, Iraq, and Iran makes us pause to consider whether we remain "all for Jesus" as they were (see "Real-life Stories" reading list in appendix 2).

---

[54] DC Talk and The Voice of the Martyrs, *Jesus Freaks: Stories of Those Who Stood for Jesus: The Ultimate Jesus Freaks* (Tulsa: Albury, 1999), 16.

In our day believers in various parts of the world face suffering with the same attitude of faith as those who have gone before. At mission conferences I have heard Christians from the developing world comment: "Humanly speaking, we know that no one likes to suffer physically. But I know that if the Lord leads me into it, He will give me the strength to survive it." A Vietnamese Christian captured the spirit of steadfast faith in the face of death when he said, "Suffering is not the worst thing that can happen to us. Disobedience to God is the worst thing." As C. S. Lewis wrote, "You never know how much you really believe anything until its truth or falsehood becomes a matter of life and death to you."[55] Christians face this reality every day somewhere in our world.

Individual abilities and leadings from God may vary tremendously, but all Christians are called to yield their lives unreservedly to God for His purposes. Dietrich Bonhoeffer's admonition in *The Cost of Discipleship* resonates with believers of every generation: "When Christ calls a man, he bids him come and die."[56] From the first century to the present day, men and women have gladly sacrificed their all for the sake of Jesus and His kingdom.

The church today must present the biblical call to discipleship that recognizes and embraces God's work in redemption. It should not be surprising that young people lack conviction about giving themselves to cross-cultural work if they have not been exposed to the biblical theme of God's desire to reach the world through His people. Christians need to be exhorted to remember afresh the holiness of God and the hopelessness of those who fail to respond to Him.

In addressing the question of fear in regard to cross-cultural ministry, mention must be made of the influence of the news and social media. The surveys demonstrated that knowledge of and responses to other cultures and worldviews have often been shaped by what is

---

[55] C. S. Lewis, *God in the Dock: Essays on Theology and Ethics* (Grand Rapids: Eerdmans, 1970), 52.

[56] Dietrich Bonhoeffer, *The Cost of Discipleship*, 1st Touchstone ed. (New York: Touchstone, 1995), 99.

circulating in the media. Although the media is an easy target, and on a positive note does provide connections to the world outside our limited parochial bubble, it can misinform, sensationalize, and mislead.

As a twenty-something myself, I was slow to realize that not all media reports are accurate or reliable. My confidence in news reporting was shattered during my time in Vietnam. At that point in history, the American media and the public were growing antagonistic towards the war (a position with which I later came to concur). While I was stationed on a landing zone called Ross in South Vietnam, our unit was attacked at night. We were vastly outnumbered by the brigade-level North Vietnamese Army and pinned down, although eventually we repelled the attack. The NVA never entered our perimeter, but caused numerous casualties with small arms fire, mortars, and rockets. But, according to my parents in the USA, the *Huntley Brinkley Report* evening news claimed that Landing Zone Ross had been attacked and "overrun, with catastrophic casualties." A *Time* magazine article stated the same. My parents were convinced I had died based on these dire, but incorrect, reports.

The news reports made grossly inaccurate statements. In military terms, "overrun" means the enemy breaks through a perimeter and moves over the beaten opponent's camp, exiting at the other side. The dictionary defines "overrun" as "to swarm over in great numbers." This never happened at LZ Ross, contrary to the media statements. This experience opened my eyes to the exaggeration and bias possible in news reporting. The Millennial generation seems more aware of this and has adopted an attitude of distrust bordering on cynicism in regard to much of what comes through the news media. Many of them see media attacks on Muslims to be as undeserved as the Islamic world's portrayal of all American women as promiscuous based on movies and television.

In contrast to previous generations, social media has become all important to these young people. The ease of blogging, posting video to "You Tube," "Facebooking," texting, and "tweeting" has opened a Pandora's box of unfounded rumors and opinions that make the rounds, often unquestioned. A comment with no basis in fact is passed from person to person and accepted as the truth, usually without any attempt to validate its source or accuracy. The possibilities for distortion and misunderstanding are immense. Millennials react with horror to what they see as stereotypes, but tend to uncritically accept what comes to them via social media, even though it may be stereotype or downright error.

The centrality of the social media in the lives of this generation stood out starkly this week as we write. After the Boston Marathon bombing on Monday, law enforcement officials posted security camera video of the two suspects and requested that anyone who recognized them or had any information should call a national FBI tip-line number, which was shown on television and the Internet. Later in the week, after they were identified, one of the suspects was killed in a firefight with police, and as a huge manhunt was underway to find the other, we watched various friends and classmates of the nineteen-year-old fugitive being interviewed. One after the other, they explained, "I saw the video and thought it was Dhokar. I texted/tweeted/posted on Facebook with some of my friends, and we looked in our yearbooks to find pictures of him. We went, oh, no, it's him!"

When the interviewers would ask, incredulous, "Why didn't you call the police or the tip line?" each one answered with a variation of "Well, we weren't sure who to call . . . We didn't want to say unless we were positive, because he's not the kind of guy who would do this." Although they circulated comments and rumors via social media for days, in the world of reality they took no action.

In one of the incongruities observed in the Millennial generation, although they depend on the social media for both knowledge and interaction, they prefer firsthand experience with people or a situation to being told or expected to accept someone else's analysis. One of the students we interviewed said, "The best way to overcome stereotypes and a lack of understanding is often to experience people or practices which are contradictory to the stereotypical perception." This is why short-term missions have become a necessary part of current mission strategy. A short-term experience is frequently more about change in the person who goes than about actual work accomplished. My research and personal comments of students attest to the value of short-term experiences in reducing fear and changing misconceptions about people unlike ourselves. Interacting with the "other" allows this generation to see the individuals behind the mass religious identity.

Despite the fact that some aspects of Greg Mortenson's work in Pakistan have been criticized, some of his stories have an authentic ring for those who have traveled or ministered in this area. One story that sounds credible took place on Friday, September 14, 2001, three days after the World Trade Center attack. Mortenson and a colleague drove to Kuardu to participate in the scheduled inauguration of the first primary school built through his efforts and those of local Pakistanis. The school was open and beginning to educate the local children. The celebratory event had been postponed until a date when sufficient numbers of important Pakistani officials could be present. The venue was packed. The featured speaker was the supreme Muslim leader in Baltistan, Syed Abbas. In light of the events of 9/11, everyone was prepared to listen carefully to his every word.

> "It is by fate that Allah the Almighty has brought us together in this hour," Syed Abbas said. "Today is a day that your children will remember forever and tell their children and grandchildren. Today, from the darkness of illiteracy, the light of education shines bright. We share in the sorrow as people weep and suffer in America today," he said. "Those who committed this evil act against the innocent, the women and children, to create thousands of widows and orphans do not do so in the name of Islam. By the grace of Allah the Almighty, may justice be served upon them . . . Why have we not been able to bring education to our children on our own? I request America to look into our hearts," Abbas continued, his voice straining with emotion, "and see that the great majority of us are not terrorists, but good and simple people." Later Mortenson said the entire crowd was in tears as Abbas finished his speech.

Many widows lined up to offer Mortenson and his colleague their condolences, and eggs, begging them to carry
"these tokens of grief to the faraway sisters" they longed to
comfort themselves, the widows of the New York village.[57]

We've grown up with more exposure to diverse people.
Some of my high school friends were Muslims, and I've
had the chance to visit a mosque or two. Once I had the
opportunity to share my faith with a Muslim friend, and
he (another Millennial) was furious that I would presume
that Jesus was the only Savior and path to God. Strange,
since Islam makes similar exclusive claims about its creed.
It was a difficult experience because we were good friends.
SF, Millennial Blog

Is fear a factor in Millennial decisions about pursuing cross-cultural ministry, particularly in Muslim areas? Research for my earlier
book, the analysis in the April 2008 issue of *EMQ* titled "Why They
Don't Go," and the studies conducted for this book, all affirm that
fear is indeed a factor, especially in regard to comfort, security, and
family. Thinking of leaving the insulated lifestyle, abundant technology, safety, advanced health care, and limitless opportunity offered in
North America causes hesitation, the more so because there is little
encouragement in our churches towards the road of sacrificial service.
The world out there seems a threatening place due to global terrorism
and political upheaval. Overprotective and well-intentioned parents,
pastors, and friends can discourage or even outright oppose consid-
eration of a missionary career. As one mother put it, "If you go to the
mission field, you will break my heart."

I know many mission-minded peers who are excited to
follow Jesus into Muslim countries. I can count 4–5 close
friends off the top of my head (granted, I tend to hang
out with the crazies). Although we are excited to go to the

----

[57] Greg Mortenson and David Oliver Relin, *Three Cups of Tea: One Man's Mission
to Fight Terrorism and Build Nations—One School at a Time* (New York: Viking,
2006), 215–16.

hard places, I don't think we know what we're up against, exactly. This is why we need partnership with more experienced missionaries who know how to guard against discouragement and have faced persecution. However, in general, I agree that there is a fear of Muslim nations in Christian circles. *SF, Millennial Blog*

As mentioned, this is the week of the Boston Marathon bombing. Since one of the three innocent bystanders who died was a Chinese graduate student, China has been awash with "tweeting" about the event. One typical tweet claimed, "The free world is not safe!" Yet thousands of Chinese citizens will continue to flock to the West to take advantage of educational and business opportunities. Will the next generation of Christians continue to flood the spiritually imprisoned world, despite it not being safe, to give away the life and truth of Jesus? To quote China missions pioneer Hudson Taylor, "Without the element of risk in our exploits for God, there is no need for faith."

WHAT MINISTRIES INTEREST MILLENNIALS?

Basically, Millennials want to experience the world, take some risks, make an impact on both social and spiritual levels, and learn from other cultures and experienced workers!

This generation seems to have great appreciation for the current, increasingly popular "Four Worlds" model of cultural learning and influence, which highlights each region of the world's strengths and contributions to the global community. In contrast to previous generations of Western missionaries, they reject working independently from others (both nationals and missionaries) and want to see people working together at all levels. They do not appreciate "one-upmanship," where people draw attention to themselves and their own contributions. They take a cooperative, collaborative approach to work and ministry, and are interested in learning from others—especially, on the field, from local leaders and other local people.

An incident from *Three Cups of Tea* describes such a situation. Greg Mortenson was shouting out orders to try to speed up the building of a school. A local friend, Haji Ali, exhorted Mortenson to sit and listen. When he did, Haji Ali began to teach him about local customs and culturally appropriate communication. Three weeks later, "with Mortenson demoted from foreman to spectator, the walls of the school had risen higher than the American's head and all that remained was putting on the roof." Mortenson learned the first of a series of important cross-cultural lessons, beginning with the need to "make time to share three cups of tea."[58] Westerners may have a cartful

---

[58] Mortenson and Relin, *Three Cups of Tea*, 150.

of knowledge and answers, but in a new cultural context may be humbled to find that learning and effectiveness comes in what appears to be an uneducated or old-fashioned package with "Middle Eastern" or "Asian" written on it. In Mortenson's words, "An illiterate old Balti taught a Westerner how best to go about developing his 'backward' area, using relationships already established."[59]

A number of missionaries and national church leaders have mentioned to us their appreciation for Western young people who join their evangelism, discipleship, and church-planting teams. These newer workers have been trained in cultural sensitivity and demonstrate willingness to learn on the job in the local context. The local leaders often prefer to assist newcomers in what they consider the best contextual approach on the spot. Specific contextual training received outside the target locale frequently turns out to be inaccurate or mixed with misunderstandings. A cultural/local situation cannot be completely recreated in a training program, but principles of cultural adaptation can be taught. With Millennials, the tendency may be to oversensitivity when it comes to interfering with other people's cultures. In one field team I visited, recently arrived young workers were hesitant to bring out their guitars to lead believers in worship. They were concerned that "their" music style and content would be seen as "the" acceptable form of worship and would stifle local expression in music.

JUSTICE AS A DEMONSTRATION OF THE CHARACTER OF GOD

Millennials respond enthusiastically and passionately to exhortations regarding justice. One of the fastest growing North American organizations aims at moving into other cultures to develop trust/bond relationships in communities that lead into efforts to change laws and promote justice for those caught in such horrendous situations as sex trafficking. Jesus certainly spoke of and demonstrated His concern for the "least of these," and the desire to improve the lot of the

---

[59] Ibid., 177.

marginalized in society resonates with this generation. They rise to the call to act in the interest of others, feed the hungry, do justice, and love mercy. Students interviewed for our research frequently expressed their preference for showing love to the needy before attempting to present or challenge any beliefs. The young generation has a particular affinity for working with children.

> Growing up in the American church, we have seen a lot of people talk about Jesus and His love for the hurting, but we failed to see it lived out in our families or in the community. Christians are known for talking, for their political opinions, for their stance on abortion and marriage (which are important issues), but not for taking tangible steps outside their comfort zones to minister to actual people with real pain and real needs. *SF, Millennial Blog*

This comment may sound uninformed or even unfair, especially to those who have given their lives to addressing human needs of every kind, but it shows that any mission agency or other ministry hoping to attract young workers to its membership must address the implications of God's concern for justice in its fullest sense.

Biblical passages such as "Do not exploit the poor because they are poor and do not crush the needy in court, for the LORD will take up their case and will exact life for life" (Prov 22:22,23); "The righteous care about justice for the poor, but the wicked have no such concern" (Prov 29:7); and "I hate, I despise your feasts, and I take no delight in your solemn assemblies. Even though you offer me your burnt offerings and grain offerings, I will not accept them . . . Take away from me the noise of your songs; to the melody of your harps I will not listen. But let justice roll down like waters, and righteousness like an ever-flowing stream" (Amos 5:21–24 ESV) have practical application and inspiration for Millennials. They yearn to live in the way *The Message* paraphrases Isaiah 58:6–8:

> This is the kind of fast day I'm after: to break the chains of injustice, get rid of exploitation in the workplace, free the oppressed, cancel debts. What I'm interested in seeing

you do is: sharing your food with the hungry, inviting the homeless poor into your homes, putting clothes on the shivering ill-clad, being available to your own families.

In 1974 committed pastors, evangelists, and missionaries joined in the Lausanne Conference for prayer, worship, and encouragement of each other to persevere in their callings. They agreed on statements regarding biblical topics, including this one on the responsibility of Christians for social justice:

> We affirm that God is both the Creator and Judge of all people. We therefore should share his concern for justice and reconciliation throughout human society and for the liberation of men and women from every kind of oppression. Because men and women are made in the image of God, every person, regardless of race, religion, colour, culture, class, sex or age, has an intrinsic dignity because of which he or she should be respected and served, not exploited . . . Although reconciliation with other people is not reconciliation with God, nor is social action evangelism, nor is political liberation salvation, nevertheless we affirm that evangelism and socio-political involvement are both part of our Christian duty.[60]

Caring acts that fulfill this affirmation have been carried out by ministers of the gospel in every part of the world. The results have been that nonbelievers becoming willing to deviate from the rules of their local religious tradition and culture and to trust foreigners, even though they come with a message that is the antithesis of local goals and practices. Compassionate, sacrificial acts of kindness and justice have moved people from every nation. Young people are drawn to this kind of ministry.

Millennial appreciation for holism leads to eagerness to participate in such activities as building schools, teaching, providing medical help, and caring for orphans, thus demonstrating compassion while gaining

---

[60] Lausanne Committee, "The Lausanne Covenant," The Lausanne Movement, http://www.lausanne.org/covenant (accessed June 9, 2009), sec. 5.

acceptance and credibility in the community. They are all about demonstrating the goodness of God in His love for people, believing this results in irresistible attraction to Jesus.

This approach to connecting with and influencing local people is not new in the history of the spreading of the gospel. Countless missionaries have demonstrated as well as proclaimed the love of God throughout the world, and the young generation can be inspired and spurred to action by the example of their lives.[61] Showing Christlike compassion for the poor and those scorned by society has long been a Christian tradition. But ministries that refuse to take this attitude, and to act upon it, may be viewed by the young generation as irrelevant. Ministry organizations may sometimes have been too traditional, fearful of the negative caricatures associated with social and humanitarian efforts, or guilty of throwing out the baby of justice and caring concern with the bathwater of liberalism.

The younger generation of Christians understands and agrees that modernity's hope of resolving human problems through science, technology, reasons, and corporate effort is insufficient and lacks the capacity and power for serious social transformation. They believe that transcendent hope, inspired by compassionate acts and given biblical content, moves beyond hollow promises to personal and societal change. They see this process as beginning with simple and sometimes random acts of kindness as explained by Jesus, "For I was hungry and you gave me food, I was thirsty and you gave me drink, I was a stranger and you welcomed me, I was naked and you clothed me, I was sick and you visited me, I was in prison and you came to me" (Matt 25:35,36 ESV).

One profound example of such acts is buried in the twenty-six-hour miniseries, *War and Remembrance*. During World War II a trainload of Jewish prisoners is being transported to a concentration camp. Days of horror pass, people of all ages packed like sardines into boxcars with no food, no water, no sanitation, some dying of suffocation, others

---

[61] See books suggested in appendix 2.

losing their reason. At some point in this agonizing nightmare, the train pulls into a small station. The guards and engineer exit the train and go inside for refreshments. While they are distracted, a poorly dressed, anonymous old man begins shuffling along the length of the train, pulling from his basket beautiful red apples and lifting them up to the hands desperately reaching through the small barred windows. The prisoners are astounded by this moment of kindness as they have come to expect only brutality and contempt. At one point a voice calls out, "Why are you doing this?" The old man replies simply, "I am a Christian."

An example familiar to Millennials is that of Mother Teresa of Calcutta demonstrating the love of God in contrast to cultural norms. Regarding her choice to give her life to caring for people others saw as worthless, she wrote:

> When we care for a needy person we touch Jesus' suffering body, and this contact . . . makes us forget our repugnance and our natural tendencies. We need the eyes of a profound faith to see Christ in the maimed bodies and dirty clothes in which is hidden the fairest among the sons of men.[62]

> Honestly, I think this is the heart cry of so many in my generation. We are tired of mediocre faith and want to be challenged, we are disenchanted with the Church we grew in and want to live holistic, authentic lives. We want something beautiful and real. Unfortunately, we saw a lot of folks caught up in peripheral things that made the church lose its spiritual-salty-ness. We want to know who Jesus is aside from what other people have told us. We want to find out for ourselves. How is this going to make a real difference in our lives and in the lives of others? It's fine and dandy to debate theology all you want, but if you end up with an arrogant head full of knowledge without

62 Anonymous, "Mother Teresa of Calcutta," UMILTA, http://www.umilta.net/calcutta.html (accessed November 13, 2009).

love, without a true expression of Christ played out socially, in community, in the world, then you've got a head full of garbage and a heart full of the same.

I realize that not everyone groans at the idea of working in an office, but I think it's the case, more and more, that our generation seeks to move past their padded comfort zones and get their hands dirty. What is the point of working? To earn more money . . . to do what with it exactly? I'd probably travel with it . . . and tell people about Jesus and love them and care for them and try to help them and write stories about them—isn't that what a missionary does . . . so why not just begin with missions in the first place? Our generation is concerned about making a lasting difference. *SF, Millennial Blog*

HOW CAN ORGANIZATIONS AND MILLENNIALS WORK TOGETHER?

When leaders prejudge the younger generation, there is a danger of missing ministry "diamonds in the rough." Judging young people by appearance or initial presentation is similar to judging a book by its cover and can cause ministry mobilizers to miss hidden gems. I remember at the Urbana student missions conference meeting a young man who was interested in possible ministry with our agency. The first things I noticed about him were his prominent dangling earrings. After he left, planning to return the next day for further discussion, I couldn't get the picture of those earrings out of my mind. My initial reaction was to dismiss him as unsuitable. That night as I was thinking further about the young man and his appearance, the Lord reminded me of the passage in Acts 10 when the Lord speaks to Peter about his avoidance of Gentiles and tells him not to "call something unclean if God has made it clean" (v. 15 NLT). The following day I had a long discussion with the young man and was deeply moved by his love for Jesus and mature attitude to ministry. The truth is that in certain contexts our appearance may affect our work with people, particularly in some cross-cultural settings. I believed he understood and would respond appropriately. At the end of our conversation I was overwhelmed by the realization that I might have missed the work God was doing in this person due to a shortsighted judgment based on his appearance.

Millennials, church leaders, mission leaders, mobilizers, and field workers can progress toward productive integration and collaboration, allowing for the merging of each one's strengths and weaknesses. This will take understanding and flexibility on everyone's part. The younger generation does not hesitate to refuse to cooperate with leaders who appear to have little regard for new workers' ideas, contextualization, or development of local indigenous leadership. They would be reluctant to participate in any organization or ministry that seems to lack sincere commitment to the social, racial, and gender equality ideals they deem important. Older leaders need to be sensitive to even the perception of discriminatory attitudes since problems in this area can lead to a Millennial questioning the validity of an organization. Leaders must make certain they communicate and demonstrate a diversity-friendly atmosphere. Anything less than perceived authenticity, genuine truthfulness, and a straightforward approach will result in rejection by these young people.

Older generations might have put up with less than stellar leadership because of a superior's title and position in an organization, or fear of recrimination might have resulted in hesitancy to confront or refuse to submit. Not so the younger generation, who may not confront directly, but will not continue with a leader they don't believe in or trust.

Recent discussion with one young ministry worker revealed her deep disappointment over her leader's inability or unwillingness to hear the deep longings of her heart and her aspirations for authentic development. Although we know her to be an engaging, gifted person capable of significant contributions, as the result of her disillusionment she left that organization.

This generation wants leaders who are coaches rather than directors. Their preferred style is for leaders "to be very involved in my life. I love a leader who desires a 'hands-on' approach and not only sets the example by what they say, but also provides space in their schedule and life so that I can learn from being under and next to them in the ministry world . . . I also like leaders who utilize mentoring in developing new leaders." (from interviews)

Young people hold high expectations for family, including safety. They look for opportunities for strong parental engagement in children's lives. Family priorities will often come first in choices regarding geographic placement and ministry options. Discussion and interviews seem to align with the research: Millennials will evaluate institutions on how they enhance a worker's ability to fulfill his or her role as a parent, to raise children, and to provide for a household. Several interviewees mentioned the importance of a mission organization's support for raising a family in a cross-cultural context. As one said,

> I would like to say I'd be willing to live with my children in a "difficult" nation. I have a feeling that it has been more difficult to answer as I enter motherhood. It would very much depend on the support given to my family by our mission and the specific needs of my own children and their impact in the community.

Millennials want churches, mission agencies, and nonprofit organizations to develop and clearly communicate policy regarding provisions for young families. They are not content to let this area of life develop by chance, but will be intentional about examining the resources for, and attitude about, families. Their families protected and nurtured them, and they expect to eventually do the same for their children. Raising a family tops the list of life objectives that are "essential" or "very important" to Millennials—more so than for their parents' generation.

This generation tends to wait longer to marry and set up house than earlier generations, which can have both positive and negative implications for global ministry. Waiting until later in life to take on home mortgages and other debt places them in a more flexible vocational position. Living with parents longer and being reluctant to marry is viewed as being economically wise, but can also reflect fear of obligations and responsibility or desire to keep all options open. Many Millennials exhibit dependence on their parents, which may postpone the maturation milestones associated with financial independence.

Young people take for granted the use of current technology for social networking, research, reducing unnecessary work steps, and accomplishing goals. They have grown up playing Internet checkers with people around the globe and are potential catalysts for improving communication and efficiency in an organization.

This generation brings to ministry an inclusive tolerance and embracing of other races and cultures and a willingness to listen to other religious positions, along with genuine enjoyment in learning from others. They thrive on teamwork, believing a collaborative "we are smarter than me" attitude can accomplish more than working alone. As ministries here and abroad become increasingly focused on team dynamics, these young people can make a significant contribution. They have been trained to work in groups since early childhood and can be comfortable in settings where communities live and function closely together.

Millennials believe the type of career-long loyalty to a company or organization demonstrated by their parents or grandparents is not for them. If what they're involved in seems boring or not rewarding enough, they will move on rather than sticking it out. As we heard a BBC commentator state, "You mention duty to an eighteen-year-old, and he'll give you a blank look. It isn't a concept that has any currency anymore."

Their optimism, self-absorption, indulgence, and high expectations can result in a fluid and sometimes uncertain approach to work. Clare Raines reports that "as the most recent generation to enter the fray, Millennials are likely to ask their older colleagues to chill out, get a life, and walk a mile in a younger generation's shoes."[63] Our interviews confirmed that they make commitments by increment, based on a sense of bonding or feeling they are being valued by an organization. Interestingly, stability in an organization—with a comprehensible goal statement lived out in practice by its people—means a great deal to Millennials. They want to see a balance between stability and adaptability/flexibility, programs that include internships, and a history of achievement when they are considering a job or ministry.

Interviews suggest that commitment to a mission begins when Millennials sense pastoral commitment to them on the part of the

---

[63] Claire Raines, "Managing Millennials," Claire Raines Associates, http://www.generationsatwork.com/articles/Millennials.html (accessed September 13, 2009; page discontinued).

organization. They appreciate visits from supervisors that are informal; initiated by the supervisor; include listening, not primarily speaking, on the supervisor's part; and have prayer as a significant part of the interaction. These visits are often more comfortable and open for the young person when they are spontaneous, not scheduled, and when great interest in how the Millennial is doing in life and ministry is expressed.

In his study of organizational commitment, job satisfaction, and turnover of cross-cultural workers, Dr. Doug Trimble found that beyond a desire for good pastoral care, respondents "desired and valued the following from their supervisors: clear communication, verbal encouragement, respect for their opinions, inclusion in decision-making, and mentoring."[64] Millennials we interviewed expressed desire for a leader who gets close to them, emanates an attitude of openness and approachability, invites the young worker into his or her life, and believes even the newest team member can contribute to the work of the developing church as well as the missionary team. This generation wants to work among learners, not among people who think they "know it all." As one student put it, "I prefer informal/mentor type guidance, with lots of autonomy but plenty of resources and availability for further guidance. Although I see a value and place for formal structure and instruction, I'd rather a ministry team be authentic, critical thinkers who seek to learn as much as they teach."

Above all, Millennials want to see passion in their leaders to match the passion they bring to ministry themselves. A "business-as-usual" attitude is a great turnoff for this generation. Love for Jesus, passion for ministry, and ability to make room for family life are key components in what they seek in a compatible organization.

Research and interviews confirm that the young generation wants to give back to society. Participation in AmeriCorps and the Peace Corps is a popular option for some, and an immediately profitable

---

[64] Douglas E. Trimble, "Organizational Commitment, Job Satisfaction, and Turnover Intention of Missionaries," *Journal of Psychology and Theology* 34, no. 4 (2006): 358.

career is no longer the major focus of important life decisions for all aspiring young people. Many will experiment with a variety of work and ministry placements. They believe making a difference in some sphere of life is as important as their own personal success. Enjoying volunteerism has helped them develop a service mentality and a desire to contribute to the common good. For Christian young people, missions can be a logical path to follow if aspirants and appropriate organizations can meet and mesh.

A number of this generation's characteristics line up well with what mission organizations are looking for in applicants. However, others do not. Both sides will need to recognize that flexibility and adapting to each other, as well as to the people they are attempting to reach, are necessary.

POSITIVE SIMILARITIES

Millennials	*Organizations*
Want to make a difference in the world	Committed to God's purposes
Tolerant, multicultural	Not too ethnocentric
View discrimination as ignorant	See others of any background as equals
Team oriented	Able to live and work well with others
Willing to learn	Learners
Appreciate older generations' wisdom	Respect leaders
Adventurous, creative	Creative, self-starters
Comfortable with paradox, tolerant	Firm, steady faith yet willing to let go of personal opinions

AREAS WHERE MILLENNIAL ORGANIZATIONS MAY NEED TO GROW AND CHANGE

Millennials	Organizations
Feel entitled, not used to criticism, overinflated expectations	Willingness to work at whatever needs to be done, humble
Commitment in increments, like to keep options open	Commitment and perseverance for long-term work
Want clearly defined job description	Willing to work at whatever needs to be done
Expect Western amenities, including the latest technology	Willingness to live simply and to sacrifice if necessary

In light of the above, here are five practical suggestions for missions mobilizers, put together by students at Columbia International University:

1. Stay away from the traditional booth method.
2. Less focus on the agency/organization and more focus on "personal stories."
3. Share "inside details" of life in the ministry—the nitty-gritty.
4. Fun activities to interact with students—quality time versus seminars.
5. Care more about students' journeys in God's mission and less about recruitment.[65]

WHAT WOULD A MILLENNIAL'S IDEAL MISSION AGENCY LOOK LIKE?

A Millennial's ideal mission would be evangelical and demonstrate appreciation for God's work through various churches and other missionary organizations. The members and leaders would come from

---

[65] Jean Chang, "5 Suggestions for More Effective Recruitment and Mission Mobilization" (report, Columbia International University, Columbia, SC, October 2010).

various national, cultural, and ethnic groups and thus represent the fullness of the worldwide church. The organization would have a global, holistic, and strategic outlook, with the flexibility to be open to new moves of God, new ideas, and use of new technology to spread the gospel. A track record of successes, failures, working through crises, and continuing to press on to its goals would show the misson's stability, authenticity, and commitment. An honest transparency about the strengths and weaknesses of an organization and its leadership is more impressive to a Millennial than a blustery veneer of infallibility.

Discrimination would not be tolerated in this mission. Leaders would be chosen because of spiritual maturity and leadership qualities without regard for background, gender, nationality, or race. Leaders would be mentors and examples, working and serving "in the trenches" alongside their colleagues and allowing all members to know them and their families well.

The mission's training institutions and administrative centers would be residential communities, where students, applicants, and staff members would share life together and learn to solve difficulties, make group decisions, work as a team, and pray together in the most practical ways in daily life. Training and orientation courses would be long enough to allow new members to establish a strong family bond with others in the organization, resulting in permanent connectedness and strong prayer fellowship. Younger members looking for authenticity and practical outworking of faith would gain from seeing older members living sacrificially, and from interaction with those who have long experience in ministry.

Each member would be encouraged to seek God's direction for the ministry and to develop his or her gifts, abilities, and creativity. Emphasis on becoming a lifelong learner and being included in team decision making would help members to keep thinking and praying strategically rather than settling into a routine work pattern. The mission would be open to using new methods and technology, willing to change what is not working, and welcoming to the ideas and skills of every member. Wherever possible, field and ministry decisions would be made at the local/team level, not imposed from a board or hierarchy at "home."

Finally, care for missionary families and children would be in the forefront of the organization's thought and planning. Parents would be encouraged to see that their whole family is called into missions and to include their children in ministry wherever possible. Educational alternatives, parenting principles, health on the field, flexibility in placement and ministry, and other relevant topics would be presented and discussed during training and orientation so new workers could be prepared as well as possible for family life.

> Almost two years out of college and my life hadn't amounted to much. I was itching to move and go and do, which wasn't happening. So I started to freak out about my entire identity: Who am I? How can I possibly make a difference? What about my future? What if I live in a dump my entire life? What if I can't feed myself? What if I can't save for retirement? What if it's painful? What if people look down on me? What if I'm headed the wrong way? What if God forgets that I want to serve Him? What if I never get to be a missionary. What if I'm stuck at a desk my entire life? What keeps me from really loving, trusting, and giving my all for Jesus? What if all my passion and zeal is fake and what if it's only words and I'll never get to practice what I believe? What am I doing now that makes a difference? What IF it's dangerous? What IF family protection, job security, and health and retirement funds will suddenly become so important to me that I miss what God has for me? Those voices are getting pretty loud. What IF I really am naïve and everyone else is right? What IF my heart's cry to serve and help and sing of Jesus is just a young phase and I'll "grow out of it and get practical"? I can't be the first person to have these passions, then why aren't there more people who sacrifice? Who go into the wild places? Who turn their backs on the American dream? Where are these people? *SF, Millennial Blog*

Where are these people? Shasta, you probably won't see many of them here in Minnesota, because they're in Abidjan and Belo Horizonte and Kardzhali and Phnom Penh and N'Djamena and Lautoka and Dunkerque and Serrekunda and Thessaloniki and Kyoto and Morelos and a thousand other places . . . and they will rejoice if you and others with your heart go too!

MINISTRY DEAL BREAKERS FOR MILLENNIALS

The following are attitudes or situations Millennials would find unacceptable and typically would make them reluctant to join in a ministry:

1. Unwillingness to consider the young worker's ministry aspirations.
Young workers typically enter ministry with a rather extensive background of study, short-term team experience, and practical preparation. Their hearts and heads are filled with dreams of what they can do for Jesus and the kingdom. Some of their notions may be unrealistic, but one of the worst possible responses is for a leader to outright negate those aspirations or to indicate a bored unwillingness to even consider them.

2. A distorted presentation of the ministry's strengths or successes.
This generation can be skeptical of unwarranted claims and would much prefer to hear a realistic overview of the "good, bad, and ugly." Anything less may send them packing, looking for some other organization that recognizes and communicates both its strengths and its weaknesses. Similarly, an individual should not appear to give a less-than-honest description of his or her work. Undoubtedly there have been both mountaintop and valley experiences in everyone's personal history. Sharing these honestly can be a catalyst to draw Millennials closer, rather than repulsing them with a blast of "hot air."

3. Instruction rather than stories.
Lectures are boring, but Millennials love and are motivated by meaningful narratives of older missionaries' journeys and God's faithfulness.

Mission history embedded in personal stories can be inspiring to a young person. Hearing or reading of an experienced missionary's anxieties and fears, and of God's faithfulness and provision over the years, can aid in growth and commitment as well as in explaining the organization's growth and vision.

4. Second-class treatment.

Aretha Franklin sang it, and young workers want it: "Respect." When a Millennial is treated condescendingly, or older workers demonstrate or imply patronizing superiority, those of the younger generation react negatively. They expect to be treated as full members of their new organizational family. Leaders are on solid biblical ground when they take to heart Jesus' words: "Don't let anyone call you 'Rabbi,' for you have only one teacher, and all of you are equal as brothers and sisters" (Matt 23:8 NLT).

5. Lack of opportunity and scope for worship.

This generation loves to worship, and it is a major source of strength and vitality for them. They can benefit from education on the content and meaningfulness of historic hymns, but will struggle if "old" (translation: anything not immediately current) is the exclusive worship style of a mission. Older members may not completely appreciate Millennial music, but should give the younger folks opportunity to share in leading worship, thus giving them a tangible expression of respect and appreciation. Significant time should be carved out within mission activities, meetings, and conferences to allow for a variety of worship styles.

6. Immediate demand for long-term commitment.

Earlier generations of Christian workers tended to make lifelong commitments to a ministry career. Not so the Millennials. Their attitudes and the short-term revolution have altered the landscape, although veteran missionaries may scoff (one overheard comment: "My five-week trip to India on the ship was my short term!"). Of course it is true that much of the work of missions cannot be accomplished in the short term, including Bible translation, language learning, evangelism, discipleship, and church planting among resistant people groups. But there are areas where short-term workers can make meaningful contributions, for instance in construction projects and refreshment and encouragement to the local church. More importantly, short-term experience / short-term commitment can provide exposure to the needs of the world, confirmation of a call to cross-cultural life, new discovery of the Lord's faithfulness, information for home churches, and renewed perspective. At times, although Millennials make commitments in steps, after a few years they may look back and realize with surprise that they've ended up spending a longer term in a ministry than originally envisioned. Initially they will often commit to at most two- or three-year segments. When it is time to consider further service with the organization, they are likely to ask such questions as: Should I continue? Is my contribution meaningful and appreciated? Do I sense confirmation from the Lord to continue? To pressure them for a deeper or longer commitment will normally result in either a premature decision to leave or a half-hearted agreement to continue.

7. Authoritarian leaders.

Millennials have "no time for sergeants." Older generations may have gone out to the field under a fairly tight regime that demanded much of new recruits. The expectation was immediate obedience in a somewhat military style like "Yours is not to question why, yours is just to do or die." Senior workers were appalled at being asked by new workers to give reasons for why things were done a certain way. That does not work for Millennials. Although they want to learn from those with more experience, they learn best in an atmosphere that encourages them to ask "why" and to evaluate the answers. Leaders and older workers who do not listen to a new person's insights and perspectives end up with a disgruntled worker and miss opportunities to view the work through fresh eyes. Not all ideas from any generation are valid, but it is critical to maintain an environment of mutual learning and openness to new ideas and genuine concerns.

Yep, that's true of me. My mom and I used to get in pretty deep arguments because I wouldn't stop asking "Why?" I wanted to know! I wanted to understand. I wanted to challenge ideas and opinions in order to reach a better conclusion, a better method, and a better outcome. Though I strove to treat all authorities in my life with kindness and respect, the teachers I loved the most were those who treated me like a young woman with a heart and a brain. Not an "underling." They were authentic because they valued me as a teammate and a rational, caring, capable human. I think rather than seeing me as a child, they saw me as a young woman on her way to maturity, and they were helping me get there. *SF, Millennial Blog*

RECOMMENDATIONS FOR SUCCESSFUL INTEGRATION OF THIS GENERATION

First, a tip for Millennials: be aware that criticism of more senior workers can make them defensive and put them on edge. New culture and language learners need to attempt to phrase their misgivings in the form of questions, not critiques. Some ministry operations may seem archaic, but have an important cultural history that, if neglected, could set back the work of God's kingdom. Millennial appreciation for being heard needs to work both ways, and "being a learner" applies not only to national cultures, but to mission and team cultures as well.

Next, a few suggestions for ministry leaders and teams:

1. Leaders should initiate conversations with young workers to learn how to integrate them into ministry teams.
It is helpful if the team expresses a desire to understand the new workers. Studying about this generation doesn't eliminate the need to invite direct input from its members. Conversational questions that may lead to revelation about what makes these young people "tick" might include:

- Identify one of your heroes. What do you admire about him or her?
- What events shaped you during your formative years?
- What's the most interesting class you've ever taken? Why?
- What about you would surprise us?

- What, besides your family, is something you're really proud of?
- What is one of your best team skills?
- What is one thing we should make sure you're not in charge of?
- How can we help you be more successful on this team?[66]

2. Leaders should try to coach and counsel, not criticize and rebuke.
Try to find out what is behind the young worker's comments or actions. For instance, his or her demand for speed related to technology in the operation of the field is not a sign of laziness: utilizing the latest electronic tools is simply an efficiency issue. Discussion with new workers should include positive and negative, as well as always attempting to address the need for change by including their input. "What do you think could be done differently in the future?" is more effective than a lecture on what they've done wrong. Asking about what they think is working well and what is not, taking their comments seriously, and recognizing that they have fresh and insightful eyes and ears as they enter a new team or culture, is helpful. Their observations are not always wise or appropriate, but some could be useful to a team locked in the "tyranny of tradition." Being heard means a great deal to a new worker. Wise leadership will attempt to draw out a worker's thinking and heart leanings. This should be done frequently, and where possible through informal discussion over meals or coffee/tea.

3. Try to communicate the goal of church planting in line with Millennial ministry aspirations.
In our years working as training directors, we found reluctance in this young generation to engage in church planting. Ministry leaders would do well to consider how the practical elements of planting churches line up with the longings of Millennials for meaningful contributions to others. These younger workers tend to view churches as religious clubs with rules that marginalize outsiders and restrict insiders. If the true nature of the church can be communicated to them along the lines of building a community of people who love and follow

---

[66] Lynne C. Lancaster and David Stillman, *The M-factor: How the Millennial Generation Is Rocking the Workplace* (New York: HarperCollins, 2010), 239.

Jesus and care for each other as His body, Millennials may be quicker to embrace church planting.

4. Consult with younger mobilizers to gain insight into what works when talking with this generation.

Those who speak the language of youth (like The Traveling Team and SVM2, for example) can help traditional agencies with style and approaches that are appealing to Millennials. When younger aspiring missionaries are engaged and feel free to ask any questions or express their opinions without being judged or thought unspiritual, they relax and begin to feel connected. A deepening bond is created when prayer and honest concern for them are part of an encounter.

5. Be open to the possibility of preformed teams.

Increasingly Millennials are interested in joining an organization as part of a preformed team. They may have developed friendships during college or on short-term mission trips. Organizations may be hesitant about this kind of arrangement or feel that if this is encouraged, new workers may not fully integrate with members of the existing team or field. The end might be a team within a team. If the reasons are shared respectfully with new workers, they usually understand. But if the young workers' appreciation for collaborative efforts on the field are informed (not imposed, but offered as counsel) by the wisdom of more senior workers, flexibility on everyone's part can result in a "win/ win" situation.

6. Work towards building multicultural/multiethnic teams.

This generation loves diversity of thought and culture, which dovetails with the growing ministry trend toward multicultural international teams. Multiethnic teams provide a picture of the whole body of Christ and refute the assumption that Christianity is a Western, white man's religion. Millennials are willing to undergo the struggles of misunderstood communication, and cultural mistakes and adjustments, to be part of a diverse team.

7. Include parents in the process.

For many Millennials, parents are not only their closest friends, but also their most trusted confidants. They should be factored into the process of integrating the young people into a ministry organization, particularly if the applicant wants this. Authorities need to get away from feeling that parents are adversaries in the process. Leaders can assist parents in seeing both the biblical mandate to the church to "go," and the promise of God to be with their children wherever they are. Young people who sense a "calling" from the Lord will experience real anxiety if hindered from fulfilling that call by nervous parents whom they love and respect. Leading from God can provide a strong undercurrent of confidence to move forward into the unknown, even if parents misunderstand or object. But this generation certainly would prefer parents to bless and be part of the ministry pilgrimage.

8. Help new workers to find a productive niche in the ministry.

Effective work by the younger generation is related to current interest and passion. They want to be fully committed to their assigned task. Leaders will want to ensure that they are engaged in the best possible dynamic mix of the ministry's goals and the worker's vision, and to regularly make informal inquiries into the worker's attitudes about what they are doing. Although any worker may at times need to temporarily fill a critical, though personally unsatisfying, role in the team, leaders should attempt to limit these periods as much as possible. They should help the worker understand how necessary this is for the adequate functioning of the team as a whole.

As this generation joins the ministry team and begins to offer ideas for change, where possible new workers should be invited to undertake challenging activities in line with their concerns. For example, one new missionary demonstrated a particular gift in languages. This missionary was critical of the early mentoring given to her and other new arrivals on the field. She felt they were patronized and "spoon-fed" in culture and language adaptation. After her first year on the field, the team leaders decided to put this new worker in charge of the language learning process for new missionaries, with a senior worker responsible for oversight. This resulted in a successful language adaptation program and a satisfying ministry for this young missionary. New arrivals felt understood by one of their own and were more comfortable during the stressful stage of learning the language.

> Am I for real? Am I sincere? Do I have the guts to do the hard stuff? Seriously, because if not then I don't want to be fake about it, when the going gets tough, do I really have the courage to act on the love God has placed within my heart? An honest answer—no, I don't have the guts. But it was at this point where Jesus and I became really tight. I know this is what He has called me to, what He has called our generation to, what He has placed in so many of our hearts, to demonstrate our core ethos and sacrificial roots to go to all nations with the teaching and life of Jesus and share His crazy love. Jesus knows that I'm a pretty broken, selfish, cowardly young woman when you get down to it, but He still has put these desires in my heart and I need to trust Him that He's got it under control. I can be passionate and full of life, my generation can yearn for something different because it's what Jesus was about—lifting us up out of our own way and asking us to trust Him. To trust Him in seasons of rest but to walk with Him in the places of darkness. I think we'll all have to come to a point where our idealism lets us down, and the practical threatens to overwhelm us, but honestly, that's probably a good thing because then all we have is Jesus. *SF, Millennial Blog*

PERSONAL
REFLECTIONS

Will the Millennial generation be the next great wave of Christian workers? Attempting to forecast the future is not easy, or even necessarily productive. Endeavoring to predict whether the younger generation will succeed or fail in kingdom-building efforts is problematic. Questions abound.

Ministry leaders are concerned that the escalating pressure in Western society toward unbiblical tolerance, beyond the legal and neighborly, will undermine this generation's resolve to stand for truth. Millennials disdain appearing presumptuous in their knowledge and lifestyle. They do not want to appear dogmatic or unyielding in their opinions or beliefs.

Another worry is whether the self-esteem culture prevalent in the West may erode a sense of obligation and responsibility in young people. Researchers wonder if this entitled group will be able to accept the sacrifice necessary to set aside potentially lucrative futures and the comforts of the affluent life in order to serve. Is it reasonable to hope the self-indulgence acknowledged by this generation can be replaced by self-control and commitment?

Are Christian Millennials being taught biblical absolutes? Do they hold solidly to these? Do they understand that right and wrong sometimes oppose tolerance? Do their friends' opinions matter more than truth? Is the greatest sin in their eyes being critical of other people's choices?

This young generation affirms certain postmodern positions:

1. Modernity and science do not satisfy the deep needs of humans or always move us in the direction of progress.

2. Community and relationships are more important than profit, power, or success in providing meaning to life.

3. There is mystery in the universe. A worldview that includes transcendent reality is preferred over one that is mechanistic. Humility is an appreciated characteristic because it epitomizes the limits of our knowledge.

4. Everyone carries subjective presuppositions. Our personal worldview, formed by family and culture, interprets and translates all our life experiences, sometimes blinding us to diverse perspectives. The way we perceive the world is the result of our individual and shared experience. We are not blank slates, and some of what has influenced us is skewed.

Young people aspiring to ministry in a postmodern generation believe effectiveness lies as much in style and attitude as in content. Many prefer demonstration of the gospel over proclamation. Quite a few of the missionary candidates we trained and evaluated stated that they would rather just love someone than tell him or her what to believe. A statement attributed to St. Francis of Assisi, which this generation frequently repeats, is: "Preach the gospel at all times; when necessary, use words." The problem, as I often suggest in my college classes, is that if we only "live" our faith, without communicating the content upon which it is based, people conclude only that we are good people. That may be a place to start, but it is not sufficient to bring anyone to knowledge of God or to faith (Rom 10:11–15).

Aida Spencer illustrates this from her experience:

> When I was a community organizer among Hispanic Americans in New Jersey . . . the director of Adult Education, the director of the YWCA (who was Jewish), and a prominent Hispanic woman came to compliment me on my work as an organizer. I knew then that if my actions remained uninterrupted, I would simply get credit as a "good person." I replied, in much fear and trembling, "The reason I am a good community organizer is because I am a Christian." That statement caused a pause in the

conversation, but then one of the women replied, "Because I have seen your actions, I take seriously your claims."[67]

Our experience with Millennials in ministry contexts leads us to conclude that they embrace biblical absolutes personally, but are uncomfortable being seen as narrow-minded or judgmental. Does this limit their ability to speak into the lives of those living contrary to God's ways? Are they open to learning how to maintain and communicate their convictions in a manner that builds up rather than tears down? Can they learn to appreciate the Holy Spirit's conviction of sin in a person's life as His work, not theirs?

> We have a real hard time with patience: patience to not judge those who are judgmental. It's utterly frustrating to work with people/organizations who are "stuck in their ways," "unyielding" . . . if you are a passionate, loving Millennial, it can be boring and agonizing. *SF, Millennial Blog*

Will ministry supervisors be able to provide the life coaching and mentoring sought by the Millennial generation? Will older leaders respond positively to those who ask "why" frequently? Will they recognize that simply berating new workers results only in high turnover and attrition? Can generations educated in the methodology that "teaching is telling, and learning is listening" adapt to different methods of training, including team projects and one-on-one, task-oriented events?

What effect will increasing expectations for benefits associated with a job or organization have on the decision making of Millennials considering ministry careers? What about the astronomical expense of tuition and the debt incurred by graduation time? Many students and their parents prioritize debt reduction as their first goal following college, even though they have majored in cross-cultural studies and are open to God's call to missions.

---

[67] Aída Besançon Spencer and William David Spencer, eds., *The Global God: Multicultural Evangelical Views of God* (Grand Rapids: Baker Books, 1998), 24.

These questions and others remain unanswered at present, but will affect the future of Great Commission work locally and globally as the Millennials come of age.

Working with young people is inspiring and energizing. The enthusiasm, passion, quirkiness, ardor, and conviction they bring prompt us to ongoing learning and effort to avoid personal stagnation. Their creativity and constant questions cause teachers and leaders to either stonewall the inquirers or seriously consider their concerns, recognizing that we all see and "know in part" (1 Cor 13:12).

Young people who love Jesus tend to follow others who do the same, not in the name of an organization, but of the Savior. They want to see biblical knowledge matched and demonstrated by the transformed lives of Christlike people. They are particularly put off by harsh, seemingly arbitrary leaders, who are full of knowledge but show little love and humility. The following story illustrates Millennial feeling in this regard:

> A friend recently told me about his uncle, who, on retirement, decided to read right through the Bible from beginning to end in a single year. Twelve months later, having easily achieved his goal, he reasoned that with all the spare time he had on his hands, he might actually be able to read the entire book in a single month. That was a considerably more ambitious target—but he did it. Rarely has anyone been so immersed in the Bible as that man. "And here's the irony," said my friend, "my uncle died shortly afterwards . . . the meanest, bitterest son of a gun you could ever wish to meet." It's the tragic story of too many Christians and churches soaked in Scripture, yet in the end completely untouched.[68]

Spiritual reality, clothed in Christians of all generations and nationalities, has long been the desire of the people of God. A century ago mission pioneer and WEC founder, C. T. Studd, wrote:

---

[68] Chris Webb, *The Fire of the Word: Meeting God on Holy Ground* (Downers Grove, IL: IVP Books, 2011).

> I have no ambition to start another water-logged craft in the huge stream of Central Africa, but to evangelize the world and have Christ back . . . I am persuaded that when we see out duty as it is written plainly over the New Testament, and go in to perform it, we shall have a chance to glorify God. But, if not, I am equally convinced that we shall be just one more humdrum mission society, and had better never have started out thus upon God.[69]

Will this generation see its plainly written duty, go beyond its comfort zone, and respond to the biblical mandate to bring the light of God's truth to every nation? Many young people we have worked with, taught, and learned from over the years share this spirit. Based on both research and personal conduct, we are full of hope that Millennial believers can become the next great "sleeping giant" to awake and join in the task of reaching the world for Jesus.

"Great is the LORD, and greatly to be praised, and his greatness is unsearchable. One generation shall commend your works to another, and shall declare your mighty acts" (Ps 145:3,4 ESV).

---

[69] C. T. Studd, *Fool and Fanatic?*, ed. Jean Walker (Gerrards Cross, England: WEC Publishing, 1976), 18.

APPENDIX ONE

OTHER AUTHOR WRITINGS

Jim:

"How Can I Share My Faith and Encourage Others to Adopt the Biblical Worldview?" (coauthor with Dale R. Hutchcraft). In *Christian Contours*, edited by Douglas S. Huffman, 127–42. Grand Rapids: Kregel, 2011.

Marching to a Different Drummer: Rediscovering Missions in an Age of Affluence and Self-interest. Fort Washington, PA: Christian Literature Crusade, 1996.

"Reflections on Missionary Malaise." *Evangelical Missions Quarterly* (October 1997): 442–46.

Judy:

Beyond the Edge. Fort Washington, PA: CLC, 2012 (associate editor; author of "Through the Flames," "A Scary Step of Faith," "Brothers," "Safety," and "Epilogue").

Meeting Jesus in Australia. Fort Washington, PA: WEC, 1990.

"Supporting the Caregiver." In *Let All the Children Come*, edited by Phyllis Kilbourn. Fort Washington, PA: CLC, 2013.

"WEC International and the World's Cities." In *Urban Mission*, edited by Harvie Conn. Philadelphia: Westminster Theological Seminary, 1998.

(We've both written a number of articles for WEC magazines: *Worldwide Thrust* and *WEC.go*.)

APPENDIX TWO

REAL LIFE STORIES

From and about people sold out to Jesus, past and present

Bardsley, John. *He Gives Us Authority.* Gerrards Cross, England: WEC Press, 2012.

Beeson, Ray, and Ranelda Mack Hunsicker. *The Hidden Price of Greatness.* Wheaton: Tyndale House, 1991.

Broomhall, A .J. *Hudson Taylor and China's Open Century.* 5 vols. Sevenoaks, UK: Hodder & Stoughton / OMF, 1981.

Chevreau, Guy. *We Dance Because We Cannot Fly.* Tunbridge, England: Sovereign World, 2002.

Davies, Evan. *Whatever Happened to C. T. Studd's Mission?* Gerrards Cross, England: WEC Press, 2012.

———, ed. *Beyond the Edge: 100 Stories of God's Faithfulness.* Fort Washington, PA: WEC/CLC, 2012.

Dinnen, Stewart, and Marie Dinnen. *Rescue Shop within a Yard of Hell.* Christian Focus, Fearn, Scotland. 2000.

Elliot, Elisabeth. *A Chance to Die.* Old Tappan, NJ: Fleming H. Revell, 1981.

Goforth, Rosalind. *Climbing.* Wheaton: Zondervan, 1946.

Grubb, Norman. *C. T. Studd.* Fort Washington, PA: CLC, 1933, 1982, 1985.

Hale, Thomas. *Don't Let the Goats Eat the Loquat Trees.* Grand Rapids: Zondervan, 1986.

———. *The Far Side of Liglig Mountain.* Waynesboro, GA: OM, 1989.

Harveson, Stuart. *God's Orphans in Vietnam.* London: Lutterworth, 1971.

Hill, Brad. *Soul Graft.* Chicago: Covenant, 1998.

————. *Slivers from the Cross.* With Ruth Hill. Chicago: Covenant, 1990.

Magnusson, Sally. *The Flying Scotsman.* New York: Quartet Books, 1981.

Moules, Leonard C. J. *Some Want It Tough.* London: CLC, 1961.

Roseveare, Helen. *Digging Ditches.* Gerrards Cross, England: WEC / Christian Focus, 2005.

————. *He Gave Us a Valley.* Downers Grove, IL: InterVarsity Press, 1976.

————. *Living Faith.* Chicago: Moody Press, 1981.

————. *Living Holiness.* London: Hodder & Stoughton, 1986.

————. *Living Sacrifice.* Minneapolis: Bethany House, 1979.

Snyder, C. Albert. *On a Hill Far Away.* Indianapolis: Light & Life, 1995.

Steer, Roger. *Hudson Taylor: A Man in Christ.* Singapore: OMF, 1990.

Taylor, Mrs. Howard. *The Triumph of John and Betty Stam.* Philadelphia: China Inland Mission, 1935.

Woodbridge, John D., ed. *Ambassadors for Christ.* Chicago: Moody Press, 1994.

Yoo, Byun Kook. *Untold Stories of Missionary Yoo.* Gerrards Cross, England: WEC, 2009.

BIBLIOGRAPHY

Aceh. "The Rise of Islamic Conservatism in Aceh." Women Living Under Muslim Laws. http://www.wluml.org/english/newsfulltxt.shtml (accessed December 12, 2009; page discontinued).

Adeney, Bernard T. *Strange Virtues: Ethics in a Multicultural World.* Downers Grove, IL: InterVarsity Press, 1995.

Ahrend, Todd. "Overview: The Traveling Team." The Traveling Team. http://www.thetravelingteam.org/overview (accessed September 3, 2009; page discontinued).

Allen, Jimmy. *Burden of a Secret: A Story of Truth and Mercy in the Face of AIDS.* Nashville: Moorings, 1995.

Anderson, Walt. *The Truth About the Truth: De-Confusing and Re-Constructing the Postmodern World*, A New Consciousness Reader. New York: Putnam, 1995.

Anonymous. "Mother Teresa of Calcutta." UMILTA. http://www.umilta.net/calcutta.html (accessed November 13, 2009).

Bell, Rob. *Velvet Elvis: Repainting the Christian Faith.* Grand Rapids: Zondervan, 2005.

Bonhoeffer, Dietrich. *The Cost of Discipleship.* 1st Touchstone ed. New York: Touchstone, 1995.

Bosch, David Jacobus. *Transforming Mission: Paradigm Shifts in Theology of Mission.* American Society of Missiology Series, no. 16. Maryknoll, NY: Orbis Books, 1991.

Buckingham, Jane. "Ministry to Millennials: Understanding and Reaching the Next Generation." GCI Generations Ministries. http://genmin.wcg.org/Webpercent20Documents/Millennials.pdf (accessed August 19, 2009; page discontinued).

CBS News. "The 'Millennials' Are Coming." *60 Minutes*, February 11, 2009 (originally broadcast on November 11, 2007). http://www.cbsnews.com/stories/2007/11/08/60minutes/main3475200.shtml (accessed May 2, 2009).

Central Asia Institute. "Statement of Purpose and Strategy." Central Asia Institute. https://ikat.org/about-cai/history/ (accessed May 5, 2008; article discontinued).

Chacour, Elias, and David Hazard. *Blood Brothers*. Grand Rapids: Chosen Books, 1984.

Chang, Jean. "5 Suggestions for More Effective Recruitment and Mission Mobilization." Report presented at Columbia International University, Columbia, SC, October 2010.

Chester, Eric. "Generational Comparison Chart: Attitudes and Influences of Adolescence." Generation Why. http://www.generationwhy.com/articles-and-information/generational-comparison-chart.html (accessed September 28, 2009; site discontinued).

Christianity Today Weblog. "Mission Work Slows in Muslim Countries." *Christianity Today*. http://www.christianitytoday.com/ct2001octoberweb-only/10–22–32.0.html (accessed June 27, 2008).

Conn, Harvie M. *Planting and Growing Urban Churches: From Dream to Reality*. Grand Rapids: Baker Books, 1997.

Cooperrider, David L., and Diana Kaplin Whitney. *Appreciative Inquiry: A Positive Revolution in Change*. San Francisco: Berrett-Koehler, 2005.

Correll, Thomas. "Language, Christianity, and Change in Two Eskimo Communities." Address at the Symposium on the Impact of Western Ideas on Traditional Societies, University of Rhode Island, 1971.

Corwin, Gary. "Ten Things Worth Knowing about Islam." *Evangelical Missions Quarterly* 40, no. 4 (October 2004): 416–17.

DC Talk, and The Voice of the Martyrs. *Jesus Freaks: Stories of Those Who Stood for Jesus; The Ultimate Jesus Freaks*. Tulsa: Albury, 1999.

Dearborn, Tim. *Beyond Duty: A Passion for Christ, a Heart for Mission.* Monrovia, CA: MARC, 1997.

DeYoung, Curtiss Paul. *Coming Together: The Bible's Message in an Age of Diversity.* Valley Forge, PA: Judson, 1995.

Disalvo, David. "How Did Generational Differences Go from 31 Flavors to Vanilla?" True/Slant, January 8, 2010. http://trueslant.com/daviddisalvo/2010/01/08/how-did-generational-differences-go-from-31-flavors-to-vanilla/ (accessed January 9, 2010).

Donnison, Sharn. "Unpacking the Millennials: A Cautionary Tale for Teacher Education." Edith Cowan University. http://ajte.education.ecu.edu.au/ISSUES/PDF/323/Donnison.pdf (accessed July 12, 2009; page discontinued).

Dretke, James. "Islam Grows into a Strong Presence in America." Arabic Bible Outreach Ministry. http://www.arabicbible.com/christian/islam_in_america.htm (accessed December 16, 2009; page discontinued).

Du Mez, Kristin Kobes. "Plagues, Terrorism, Recessions and Christian Witness." http://www.gospelandculture.org (accessed November 23, 2010; site discontinued).

Dyrness, William A. *The Earth Is God's: A Theology of American Culture.* Faith and Cultures Series. Maryknoll, NY: Orbis Books, 1997.

Elmore, Tim. "A Generation of Paradox: The Strange Contradictory Characteristics of Generation Y." Growing Leaders. http://www.growingleaders.com/index.php?home (accessed May 23, 2008; page discontinued).

Emerson, Michael O., and Christian Smith. *Divided by Faith: Evangelical Religion and the Problem of Race in America.* New York: Oxford University Press, 2000.

Emerson, Ralph Waldo. "Ralph Waldo Emerson: Texts." Jone Johnson Lewis. http://www.emersoncentral.com/selfreliance.htm (accessed January 23, 2010).

Engel, James F., and William A. Dyrness. *Changing the Mind of Missions: Where Have We Gone Wrong?* Downers Grove, IL: InterVarsity Press, 2000.

Erickson, Don Corliss. "Northwestern College and Media Trustee Dashboard." Roseville, MN: Northwestern College, 2009.

Erickson, Millard J. *Truth or Consequences: The Promise and Perils of Postmodernism.* Downers Grove, IL: InterVarsity Press, 2001.

Escobar, Samuel. *The New Global Mission: The Gospel from Everywhere to Everyone; Christian Doctrine in Global Perspective.* Downers Grove, IL: InterVarsity Press, 2003.

Ford, Kevin Graham, and Jim Denney. *Jesus for a New Generation: Putting the Gospel in the Language of Xers.* Downers Grove, IL: InterVarsity Press, 1995.

Friedman, Thomas L. *The World Is Flat: A Brief History of the Twenty-first Century.* New York: Farrar, Straus & Giroux, 2005.

Garson, David G. "Ethnographic Research." NC State University. http://faculty.chass.ncsu.edu/garson/PA765/ethno.html (accessed June 11, 2009; page discontinued).

Generational Imperative. "America's Generations." Generational Imperative. http://www.genimperative.com/AmericasGenerations.html (accessed November 15, 2009; article discontinued).

Gibbs, Eddie, and Ryan K. Bolger. *Emerging Churches: Creating Christian Community in Postmodern Cultures.* Grand Rapids: Baker Academic, 2005.

Gladwell, Malcolm. *The Tipping Point: How Little Things Can Make a Big Difference.* Boston: Back Bay Books, 2002.

Glaser, Barney G. "Remodeling Grounded Theory." With the assistance of Judith Holton. Forum: Qualitative Social Research, May 2004. http://www.qualitative-research.net/index.php/fqs/article/viewArticle/607/1315 (accessed June 4, 2009).

Glass, Amy. "Understanding Generational Differences for Competitive Success." *Industrial and Commercial Training* 39, no. 2 (2007): 98–103. http://www.emeraldinsight.com/Insight/ViewContentServlet?Filename=Published/EmeraldFullTextArticle/Articles/0370390204.html (accessed July 27, 2009).

Greer, Robert. *Mapping Postmodernism: A Survey of Christian Options.* Downers Grove, IL: InterVarsity Press, 2003.

Guthrie, Stan. *Missions in the Third Millennium: 21 Key Trends for the 21st Century.* Waynesboro, GA: Paternoster, 2000.

Hegasy, Sonja. "Islam in the Media: Neo-orientalizing Images." The American Muslim, February 12, 2006. http://www. theamericanmuslim.org/tam.php/features/articles/islam_in_ the_media_neo_orientalizing_images/ (accessed August 10, 2009).

Henry, Carl F. H. "Theology of Mission and Changing Political Situations." In *Theology and Mission: Papers and Responses Prepared for the Consultation on Theology and Mission, Trinity Evangelical Divinity School, School of World Mission and Evangelism, March 22–25, 1976,* edited by David J. Hesselgrave, 275–91. Grand Rapids: Baker Book House, 1978.

Heskett, Jim. "How Will Millennials Manage?" Harvard Business School, August 2, 2007. http://hbswk.hbs.edu/item/5736. html (accessed December 24, 2009).

Hesselgrave, David J. *Paradigms in Conflict: 10 Key Questions in Christian Missions Today.* Grand Rapids: Kregel, 2005.

———. *Today's Choices for Tomorrow's Mission: An Evangelical Perspective on Trends and Issues in Missions.* Grand Rapids: Zondervan, 1988.

Hickman, Claude. *Live Life on Purpose: God's Purpose, Your Life, One Journey.* Eunumclaw, WA: WinePress, 2005.

Hicks, Rick, and Kathy Hicks. *Boomers, Xers, and Other Strangers: Understanding the Generational Differences That Divide Us.* Wheaton: Tyndale House, 1999.

Hiebert, Paul G. *Anthropological Reflections on Missiological Issues.* Grand Rapids: Baker Books, 1994.

Hofstadter, Richard. *Anti-intellectualism in American Life.* New York: Knopf, 1963.

Hopler, Thom, and Marcia Hopler. *Reaching the World Next Door: How to Spread the Gospel in the Midst of Many Cultures.* Downers Grove, IL: InterVarsity Press, 1993.

Howe, Neil, and William Strauss. *Millennials Rising: The Next Great Generation.* New York: Vintage Books, 2000.

Huntington, Samuel P. *The Clash of Civilizations and the Remaking of World Order.* New York: Simon & Schuster, 1996.

Jenkins, Philip. *The Next Christendom: The Coming of Global Christianity.* New York: Oxford University Press, 2007.

Johnstone, Patrick J. *The Church Is Bigger Than You Think: Structures and Strategies for the Church in the 21st Century.* Pasadena: Christian Focus, 1998.

————. *Operation World,* 21st Century ed. Waynesboro, GA: Paternoster, 2001.

————. "September 11 Prompts Sober Missions Thinking." *Christianity Today,* August 2002. http://www.christianityto-day.com/ct/2002/augustweb-only/8-26-51.0.html (accessed June 28, 2008).

Jones, Robert P., Daniel Cox, and Thomas Banchoff. *A Generation in Transition: Religion, Values, and Politics among College-age Millennials; Findings from the 2012 Millennial Values Survey.* Washington, DC: Public Religion Research Institute and Georgetown University's Berkley Center for Religion, Peace, and World Affairs, 2012. http://publicreligion.org/site/wp-content/uploads/2012/04/Millennials-Survey-Report.pdf (accessed July 7, 2012).

Joshua Project. "Where Are We? A Reflection on the Current Status of Reaching the Unreached." U.S. Center for World Mission. http://www.joshuaproject.net/swf/WhereAreWe.swf (accessed December 22, 2009; page discontinued).

Katz, Elihu, Martin L. Levin, and Herbert Hamilton. "Traditions of Research on the Diffusion of Innovation." *American Sociological Review* 28, no. 2 (1963): 237–52.

Kelley, Raina. "Generation Me." *Newsweek,* April 4, 2009.

Kimball, Dan. *They Like Jesus but Not the Church: Insights from Emerging Generations.* Grand Rapids: Zondervan, 2007.

King, Martin Luther, Jr. *Stride toward Freedom: The Montgomery Story Papers.* New York: Harper, 1958.

Kinnaman, David. "Research on Youth and Spirituality." The Barna Group. http://www.barna.org (accessed December 23, 2009; article discontinued).

Kraft, Charles H. *Anthropology for Christian Witness.* Maryknoll, NY: Orbis Books, 1996.

Kruse, Michael. "Introduction to Generational Thinking." Kruse Kronicle, December 7, 2005. http://krusekronicle.typepad.com/kruse_kronicle/2005/12/generations_pos.html (accessed December 19, 2009).

Lancaster, Lynne C., and David Stillman. *The M-factor: How the Millennial Generation Is Rocking the Workplace.* New York: HarperCollins, 2010.

Lausanne Committee. "The Lausanne Covenant." The Lausanne Movement. http://www.lausanne.org/covenant (accessed June 9, 2009).

Lewellen, Ted C. *The Anthropology of Globalization: Cultural Anthropology Enters the 21st Century.* Westport, CT: Bergin & Garvey, 2002.

Lewis, C. S. *God in the Dock: Essays on Theology and Ethics.* Grand Rapids: Eerdmans, 1970.

Long, Jimmy. *Generating Hope: A Strategy for Reaching the Postmodern Generation.* Downers Grove, IL: InterVarsity Press, 1997.

Magnuson, Doug. "Fulfilling the Mission of Bethel Seminary (to Muslims) in the Post 9-11 World." Address at Bethel Theological Seminary, MN. November 3, 2003.

McCallum, Dennis. *The Death of Truth.* Minneapolis: Bethany House, 1996.

McDowell, Bruce A., and Anees Zaka. *Muslims and Christians at the Table: Promoting Biblical Understanding among North American Muslims.* Phillipsburg, NJ: P&R Publishing, 1999.

McKnight, Scot. "Five Streams of the Emerging Church: Key Elements of the Most Controversial and Misunderstood Movement in the Church Today." *Christianity Today*, January 19, 2007. http://www.ctlibrary.com/ct/2007/february/11.35.html (accessed January 19, 2007).

Miller, Donald. *Blue Like Jazz: Nonreligious Thoughts on Christian Spirituality*. Nashville: Thomas Nelson, 2003.

Montgomery, Robert L. *The Diffusion of Religions: A Sociological Perspective*. Lanham, MD: University Press of America, 1996.

Moreau, Scott A. "Putting the Survey in Perspective." In *Missions Handbook: US and Canadian Christian Ministries Overseas 2004–2006*, edited by Dotsey Welliver and Minnette Northcutt. Wheaton: Evangelism and Missions Information Service, 2004.

Mortenson, Greg, and David Oliver Relin. *Three Cups of Tea: One Man's Mission to Fight Terrorism and Build Nations—One School at a Time*. New York: Viking, 2006.

Myers, Bryant. *Exploring World Mission*. Monrovia, CA: MARC, 2003.

Myers, William. *Research in Ministry: A Primer for the Doctor of Ministry Program*. Chicago: Exploration, 1993.

Neely, Alan. *Christian Mission: A Case Study Approach*. American Society of Missiology Series, no. 21. Maryknoll, NY: Orbis Books, 1995.

Neill, Stephen, and Owen Chadwick. *A History of Christian Missions*. New York: Penguin Books, 1986.

Newbigin, Lesslie. *The Gospel in a Pluralist Society*. Grand Rapids: Eerdmans, 1989.

Newell, Marvin. "Profile of Students Today: Preparing for Missionary Service." *Evangelical Missions Quarterly* 43 (2007): 326–33.

Noebel, David A. *Understanding the Times: The Religious Worldviews of Our Day and the Search for Truth*. Manitou Springs, CO: Summit, 1991.

Parker, Arthur Caswell. "Wallace Family Papers." American Philosophical Society. http://www.amphilsoc.org/library/mole/w/wallacefam.html (accessed April 29, 2009; page discontinued).

Parshall, Phil. *The Cross and the Crescent: Reflections on Christian-Muslim Spirituality.* Wheaton: Tyndale House, 1989.

Patai, Raphael. *The Arab Mind.* New York: Scribner, 1983.

Philips, Carol. "The Millennial Handbook: A Snapshot Guide to Everything Gen Y." Brand Amplitude. http://www.brandamplitude.com/Millennial_marketing/Millennial_marketing.html (accessed September 12, 2009; page discontinued).

Piper, John. *Don't Waste Your Life.* Wheaton: Crossway Books, 2004.

———. *Let the Nations Be Glad: The Supremacy of God in Missions.* Grand Rapids: Baker Books, 1993.

Pipes, Daniel. "American Attitudes toward Islam and Muslims: Which Direction?" *Daniel Pipes Blog*, April 14, 2006. http://www.danielpipes.org/blog/2006/03/american-attitudes-toward-islam-and-muslims.html (accessed February 8, 2008).

Pocock, Michael, Gailyn Van Rheenen, and Douglas McConnell, eds. *The Changing Face of World Missions: Engaging Contemporary Issues and Trends.* Grand Rapids: Baker Academic, 2005.

Raines, Claire. *Connecting Generations: The Sourcebook for a New Workplace.* Menlo Park, CA: Crisp, 2003.

———. "Managing Millennials." Claire Raines Associates. http://www.generationsatwork.com/articles/Millennials.html (accessed September 13, 2009; page discontinued).

Rambo, Lewis R. *Understanding Religious Conversion.* New Haven, CT: Yale University Press, 1993.

Raymo, Jim. *Marching to a Different Drummer: Rediscovering Missions in an Age of Affluence and Self-interest.* Fort Washington, PA: Christian Literature Crusade, 1996.

———. "Reflections on Missionary Malaise." *Evangelical Missions Quarterly* (October 1997): 442–46.

Religionfacts. "Comparison Chart: Christianity and Islam." Religionfacts. http://www.religionfacts.com/christianity/ charts/christianity_islam.htm (accessed August 12, 2009).

Rogers, Everett M. *Diffusion of Innovations.* New York: Free Press, 2003.

Rogers, Glen. *The Role of Worldview in Missions and Multi-ethnic Ministry.* Bedford, TX: Mission and Ministry Resources, 2006.

Rosen, Christine. "The Image Culture." *The New Atlantis* 10 (Fall 2005): 27–46.

Roseveare, Helen. *Living Holiness.* Minneapolis: Bethany House, 1986.

Salmon, Jacqueline L. "Churches Retool Mission Trips." *Washington Post,* July 5, 2008. http://www.washingtonpost.com/ wp-dyn/content/article/2008/07/04/AR2008070402233. html (accessed July 8, 2011).

Schensul, Jean J., Margaret D. LeCompte, G. Alfred Hess Jr., Bonnie K. Nastasi, Marlene J. Berg, Lynne Williamson, Jeremy Brecher, and Ruth Glasser. *Using Ethnographic Data.* Walnut Creek, CA: AltaMira, 1999.

Schmotzer, Jim. "The Next Next Generation: Born after 1980, the Optimistic and Community-oriented Millennials Are Your Up-and-coming Church Leaders." *Leadership Journal,* Summer 2004. http://www.christianitytoday.com/le/2004/ summer/15.65.html?start=1 (accessed July 14, 2009).

Scott, Brad. *Streams of Confusion: Thirteen Great Ideas That Are Contaminating Our Thought and Culture.* Wheaton: Crossway Books, 1999.

Shaw, Ryan. *Waking the Giant: The Resurging Student Mission Movement.* Pasadena: William Carey Library, 2006.

Sider, Ronald J. *The Scandal of the Evangelical Conscience: Why Are Christians Living Just Like the Rest of the World?* Grand Rapids: Baker Books, 2005.

Siewert, John, and John Kenyon, eds. *North American Mission Handbook.* Monrovia, CA: MARC, 1993.

Smets, Kaat. "In Need of an Update or Overdue? Re-evaluating the Political Life-cycle Model." KU Leuven. http://www.kuleuven.be/citizenship/Bruges/Smets.pdf (accessed June 18, 2008; page discontinued).

Southard, Kat. "The Millennials." MAVANetwork, January 10, 2012. http://mavanetwork.wordpress.com/2012/01/10/the-millennials/ (accessed January 15, 2012).

Spencer, Aída Besançon, and William David Spencer, eds. *The Global God: Multicultural Evangelical Views of God.* Grand Rapids: Baker Books, 1998.

Stafford, Darlene E., and Henry S. Griffis. "A Review of Millennial Characteristics and Military Workforce Implications." CNA. http://www.cna.org/sites/default/files/research/d0018211.a1.pdf (accessed May 22, 2013).

Stearns, Bill, and Amy Stearns. *2020 Vision: Amazing Stories of What God Is Doing around the World.* Minneapolis: Bethany House, 2005.

Steelcase. "Millennials Make Their Mark." Steelcase. http://www.360steelcase.com/e_article000526534.cfm?x=b11,0,w (accessed August 21, 2009; page discontinued).

Stone, Wilbur. "Change Agency Course Syllabus." Bethel Theological Seminary, St. Paul, MN, 2008.

Stott, John. "Yearnings of the Postmodern Heart." Griffeth-Thomas Lectureship, Dallas Theological Seminary, Dallas, TX, 1989.

Strauss, Anselm, and Juliet Corbin. *Basis of Qualitative Research: Grounded Theory Procedures and Techniques.* Newbury Park, CA: International Professional Publishers, 1990.

Strauss, William, and Neil Howe. *Generations: The History of America's Future, 1584 to 2069.* New York: Morrow, 1991.

Student Volunteer Movement 2. "Home Page Mission Statement." http://www.svm2.net (accessed September 10, 2009; page discontinued).

Sweeney, Richard T. "Millennial Behaviors and Demographics." New Jersey Institute of Technology. library1.njit.edu/ . . . /sweeney/

Millennials/Article-Millennial-Behaviors.doc   (accessed August 3, 2009).

Swinton, John, and Harriet Mowatt. *Practical Theology and Qualitative Research.* London: SCM, 2006.

Taylor, William David. "Portraits: William Carey." The Baptist Page. http://www.siteone.com/religion/baptist/baptistpage/Portraits/carey.htm (accessed January 16, 2010; site discontinued).

————, ed. *Too Valuable to Lose: Exploring the Causes and Cures of Missionary Attrition.* World Evangelical Fellowship, Globalization of Mission Series. Pasadena: William Carey Library, 1997.

Thornton, Philip, and Jeremy Thornton. "Why They Don't Go: Surveying the Next Generation of Mission Workers." *Evangelical Missions Quarterly* (April 2008).

Tiplady, Richard. *One World or Many?: The Impact of Globalisation on Mission.* Pasadena: William Carey Library, 2003.

————. *World of Difference: Global Mission at the Pick 'N' Mix Counter.* Carlisle, England: Paternoster, 2003.

Trimble, Douglas E. "Organizational Commitment, Job Satisfaction, and Turnover Intention of Missionaries." *Journal of Psychology and Theology* 34, no. 4 (2006): 349–60.

Trzesniewski, Kali H., and M. Brent Donnellan. "Are Today's Young People Really Different From Previous Generations?" The Jury Expert. http://www.astcweb.org/public/publication/documents/TheJuryExpertMay2009Volume21No31.pdf (accessed August 12, 2009).

Twenge, Jean M. *Generation Me: Why Today's Young Americans Are More Confident, Assertive, Entitled—and More Miserable Than Ever Before.* New York: Free Press, 2006.

————, and W. Keith Campbell. *The Narcissism Epidemic: Living in the Age of Entitlement.* New York: Free Press, 2009.

Underwood, Chuck. *The Generational Imperative: Understanding Generational Differences in the Workplace, Marketplace and Living Room.* North Charleston, SC: BookSurge, 2007.

Valente, Thomas W. "Social Network Thresholds in the Diffusion of Innovations." *Social Networks* 18, no. 1 (1996): 69–89.

———, and Rebecca L. Davis. "Accelerating the Diffusion of Innovations Using Opinion Leaders." *Annals of the American Academy of Political and Social Science* 566 (1999): 55–67.

Veith, Gene Edward. *Postmodern Times: A Christian Guide to Contemporary Thought and Culture.* Wheaton: Crossway Books, 1994.

Ver Beek, K. A. "The Impact of Short-term Missions." *Missiology* 34, no. 4 (2006): 477–95.

Webb, Chris. *The Fire of the Word: Meeting God on Holy Ground.* Downers Grove, IL: IVP Books, 2011.

WEC International Contextualization Committee. "Guidelines for Contextualization." Gerrards Cross, England: WEC International, 2009.

Winters, Rebecca. "Higher Learning." *Time*, January 26, 2004. http://www.time.com/time/magazine/article/0,9171,582350,00.html (accessed August 19, 2009).

Yaconelli, Mark. "Seven Trends to Watch in the Next Decade." Youth Specialties. http://www.youthspecialties.com/freeresources/articles/culture/seven.php (accessed August 2, 2009; page discontinued).

Zemke, Ron, Claire Raines, and Bob Filipczak. *Generations at Work: Managing the Clash of Veterans, Boomers, Xers, and Nexters in Your Workplace.* New York: AMACOM, 2000.

Zoba, Wendy Murray. "Youth Has Special Powers: The Millennial Generation May Be Uniquely Wired to Stand—and Sweat—for God." *Christianity Today*, February 5, 2001. http://www.ctlibrary.com/ct/2001/february5/10.56.html (accessed February 5, 2001).

INDEX